Critical Storytelling

Critical Storytelling

VOLUME 7

The titles published in this series are listed at *brill.com/csto*

Critical Storytelling

Experiences of Power Abuse in Academia

Edited by

Julie Hansen and Ingela Nilsson

BRILL

LEIDEN | BOSTON

The open access publication of this book, as well as the production of the Epilogue by Ingela Nilsson, have been supported by the research program Retracing Connections (https://retracingconnections.org/), funded by Riksbankens Jubileumsfond (M19-0430:1), with kind support from the Swedish Research Institute in Istanbul.

All chapters in this book have undergone peer review.

The Library of Congress Cataloging-in-Publication Data is available online at https://catalog.loc.gov

Typeface for the Latin, Greek, and Cyrillic scripts: "Brill". See and download: brill.com/brill-typeface.

ISSN 2590-0099
ISBN 978-90-04-52095-0 (paperback)
ISBN 978-90-04-52094-3 (hardback)
ISBN 978-90-04-52102-5 (e-book)

This book is printed on acid-free paper and produced in a sustainable manner.

Contents

CHAPTER 1

The Same Old Story?

An Introduction

Julie Hansen and Ingela Nilsson

Storytelling is seen by many as a universal human impulse, a way for individuals and groups to communicate experiences and make sense of life. It is also a social and cultural activity in which not everyone has an equal voice. As the Czech dissident and later president Václav Havel argued, "an examination of the potential of the 'powerless' [...] can only begin with an examination of the nature of power in the circumstances in which these powerless people operate" (Havel, 1985, p. 23). For those with a chance to make themselves heard, storytelling can be an empowering act that exposes injustice. Storytelling can forge a path toward better endings. By daring to tell our stories, we enter into a process that is larger than ourselves.

This volume of essays arose out of the courage of scholars and students to share stories of the academic workplace that are often only spoken of in hushed tones, if at all. The essays explore individual experiences as well as underlying institutional structures, providing original perspectives on bullying, sexual harassment, discrimination and other forms of power abuse in academic workplaces. Topics include the risks of unequal power relations for graduate students and junior faculty, the roles of gender and ethnicity, the negative effects of the tenure system and limited mobility, and the implications of new public management for academia.

This is not a reckoning with any particular institution, department or individual, but an examination of collective problems. Narratives like these comprise a necessary first step toward change. The culture of silence surrounding harassment and power abuse in the academic world needs to be broken, so that it will not always be the same old story, but a better narrative that we can call our own.

The academic world presents many obstacles to sharing such experiences. As some of the contributors observe, it can be difficult to overcome the misplaced sense of shame that victims of power abuse and harassment often feel, despite the fact that they have done nothing wrong.[1] The nefarious phenomenon of victim-blaming can be effectively mobilized to protect perpetrators by discrediting their victims. Shame and victim-blaming in connection with harassment are not specific to academia, yet some of the peculiarities of academic workplaces arguably present further obstacles to speaking out. As Sarah Viren (2021) notes, "academia is a hierarchical industry, one in which a small minority of those with secure jobs or tenure have huge sway over decisions about job security for the remaining majority" (para. 56). A tight and competitive job market can lead to a higher frequency of harassment (Blomberg, 2016, p. 51). Studies indicate that bullying in a workplace often does not stop until the harassed individual has left it for good (Blomberg, 2016, p. 35), but this option is not always available, or even desirable, for academic workers. Another risk factor appears to be emotional investment in one's work (Blomberg, 2016, p. 51). The fact that successful scholars tend to be devoted to their work may render them more vulnerable to exploitation and abuse.

Often there is a lack of institutional support, knowledge and transparent practices for dealing with work environment issues, even among some Human Resources departments. For those in academic leadership positions, incentives to acknowledge problems may be low (Twale & De Luca, 2008, p. 22). Researchers note that "heads of departments today hesitate to admit that harassment takes place at their workplace, as they see it as a disqualification of their own leadership abilities" (Björkqvist et al., 1994, p. 174). Some employees who file complaints face retaliation or unethical behavior on the part of the administrators and consultants entrusted with conducting investigations (Friedenberg, 2004).[2]

Yet there are compelling reasons for everyone with a stake in the academic world to speak out against power abuse. Research has documented the various consequences of workplace harassment for victims, and they include depression, anxiety, insomnia, post-traumatic stress disorder and suicide (Björkqvist et al., 1994; Blomberg, 2016). These unacceptable costs are not limited to individuals, however. Although more difficult to measure, the institutional losses for universities are undeniable, and these can spill over onto students and the quality of the education they receive, as well as overall research quality and output.

Despite solid data and the existence (in some places) of legislation and policies intended to prevent problems, many academics are sorely unequipped to recognize and deal with power abuse in their chosen profession.[3] Many believe it will never happen to them, yet research shows that "[a]nybody may become a victim, provided that the individual has less power than the tormentor" (Björkqvist et al., 1994, p. 175). The Swedish organizational psychologist Stefan Blomberg (2016) debunks a common myth about workplace bullying:

> There is a widely held idea that it is primarily people who behave in an eccentric or strange way who become targets of bullying. Our clinical

experience on this is clear, however. The majority of those targeted are strong, highly functional and successful individuals, whom others—colleagues, coworkers or supervisors—perceive as a threat. Many of those we encounter in clinical contexts describe feeling shocked when the bullying process begins, because they could have never imagined that they would fall victim to it. The idea that targets of bullying are eccentric or divergent makes an exception appear as the rule. This idea can also be fueled by our own fear. If only eccentric or divergent individuals can become targets, it may be easier to situate the risk beyond ourselves. (p. 50, authors' translation)

Of course, perpetrators and victims are only part of the story. More numerous are the bystanders who witness wrongful actions in their work environment and face a choice between turning a blind eye (complicity), joining in the destructive behavior (collaboration) or taking action to challenge it. All too often, bystanders choose complicity or collaboration.[4] Standing up for colleagues in such a situation entails risks and requires courage, but a collective effort to do so could be a catalyst for change.[5]

Collective is the key word here: the problems explored in this volume are collective in nature and call for collective solutions, requiring us to put aside competition in favor of collegial solidarity. Parker J. Palmer (2017) posits the following:

The external structures of education would not have the power to divide us as deeply as they do if they were not rooted in one of the most compelling features of our inner landscape—fear.

If we withdrew our assent from these structures, they would collapse, an academic version of the Velvet Revolution. But we collaborate with them, fretting from time to time about their "reform," because they so successfully exploit our fear. Fear is what distances us from our colleagues, our students, our subjects, ourselves. (p. 36)

At their worst, academic hierarchies can feel unsurmountable and paralyzing, particularly if one is fighting these problems alone. Yet as the voices in this volume attest, we are not alone. There is strength in numbers, and together we in the academic profession can do better than the status quo.

We are grateful to the authors who took on the challenge of putting their experiences into words. They come from a variety of geographical places and backgrounds. Some have already left academia, while others are just embarking on promising careers. Circumstances allow some to publish under their own names, while others have chosen anonymity to protect themselves or others. For every story that appears on the pages of this book, there are many more waiting to be told. We are especially grateful to those of you who contributed by sharing with us your unwritten stories, reading drafts, and offering invaluable advice and encouragement along the way. Your voices resound in this volume, too.

And now we invite you, our readers, to turn the page and begin to heed these stories. Their narrators speak to you through different forms, styles and genres. The plots and themes may already be familiar, or perhaps they will surprise you. Regardless, we hope you will contemplate alternative endings, because we believe it doesn't have to be the same old story.

Notes

1   Stefan Blomberg (2016) observes that it can be difficult to measure the frequency of workplace bullying precisely because most people do not want to categorize themselves as victims of it out of shame (p. 52).
2   For discussions of the phenomena of bullying and mobbing specifically in academic workplaces, see Keashly and Neuman (2010), Lewis (2004), Twale and De Luca (2008), Westhues (2004), Zabrodska (2013) and Zabrodska et al. (2011).
3   In recent decades, numerous academic career guides have been published, some of which have the word "survival" in their titles. They dispense advice on how to write productively, how to get published, how to get tenure, how to balance teaching and research, but most remain silent on how to cope with abuses of power.
4   For a taxonomy of the different kinds of reactions observed in connection with destructive work environments, see Thoroughgood et al. (2012).
5   A recent study found that witnesses of bullying at work who did not intervene ran a heightened risk of becoming a victim themselves (Rosander & Nielsen, 2021). For more on the role of bystanders, see Niven, Ng and Hoel (2020).

References

Björkqvist, K., Österman, K., & Hjelt-Bäck, M. (1994). Aggression among university employees. *Aggressive Behavior*, 20, 173–184.

Blomberg, S. (2016). *Mobbning på jobbet: Uttryck och åtgärder*. Studentlitteratur.

Friedenberg, J. E. (2004.) Political psychology at Southern Illinois University: The use of an outside consultant for mobbing a professor. In K. Westhues (Ed.), *Workplace mobbing in academe: Reports from twenty universities* (pp. 259–289). Edwin Mellen Press.

Havel, V. (1985). P. Wilson (Trans.). In V. Havel et al. (Eds.), *The power of the powerless: Citizens against the state in central-eastern Europe* (pp. 23–96, J. Kean, Ed.). Routledge. (Original work published 1978)

Keashly, L., & Neuman, J. H. (2010). Faculty experiences with bullying in higher education: Causes, consequences, and management. *Administrative Theory & Praxis*, *32*(1), 48–70.

Lewis, D. (2004). Bullying at work: The impact of shame among university and college lecturers. *British Journal of Guidance & Counseling*, *32*(3), 281–299.

Niven, K., Ng, K., & Hoel, H. (2020). The bystanders of workplace bullying. In S. V. Einarsen, H. Hoel, D. Zapf, & C. L. Cooper (Eds.), *Bullying and harassment in the workplace: Theory, research and practice* (3rd ed., pp. 385–408). CRC Press.

Palmer, P. J. (2017). *The courage to teach: Exploring the inner landscape of a teacher's life* (20th anniversary ed.). Jossey-Bass.

Rosander, M., & M. B. Nielsen. (2021). Witnessing bullying at work: Inactivity and the risk of becoming the next target. *Psychology of Violence*. Advance online publication. https://doi.org/10.1037/vio0000406

Thoroughgood, C. N., Padilla, A., Hunter, S. T., & Tate, B. W. (2012). The susceptible circle: A taxonomy of followers associated with destructive leadership. *The Leadership Quarterly*, *23*, 897–917.

Twale, D. J., & De Luca, B. M. (2008). *Faculty incivility: The rise of academic bully culture and what to do about it.* Jossey-Bass.

Viren, S. (2021, May 25). The native scholar who wasn't. *The New York Times Magazine.* https://www.nytimes.com/2021/05/25/magazine/cherokee-native-american-andrea-smith.html

Westhues, K. (Ed.). (2004). *Workplace mobbing in academe: Reports from twenty universities.* Edwin Mellen Press.

Zabrodska, K. (2013). Prevalence and forms of workplace bullying among university employees. *Employee Responsibilities and Rights Journal*, *25*, 89–108.

Zabrodska, K., Linnell, S., Laws, C., & Davies, B. (2011). Bullying as intra-active process in neoliberal universities. *Qualitative Inquiry*, *17*(8), 709–719.

CHAPTER 2

The Polyphony of Academia

Ingela Nilsson

An important part of my job as a university professor is listening to people's stories. Since academia is such a multicultural, inclusive and diverse environment, I hear an amazing range of voices and stories. It's an ever growing collection for which I'm running out of space. Where to put them? Will they go bad if I don't store them correctly? Should I sort them under specific categories? I need a solution, they are taking over my office, my spare time, my life. All these voices, spinning round and round in my head, urging me to listen to them:

> I read the article over and over, hoping I was mistaken, that I wasn't reading my own words under someone else's name. But to my great horror I could only conclude that I had been right from the start: this was a chapter from my dissertation, published under the name of one of my supervisors. I didn't know what to do, so I contacted my other supervisor to ask for advice. She said it was not the first time and asked me to produce evidence that the material was really mine. I spent a week digging up dated files, putting together a time line, but in the end it didn't lead to anything—the article is still out there and I had to refer to it in my thesis instead of the other way around. And now you're telling me how important it is to be open and share our work with others, how the hell am I supposed to feel about that?

> I mean, it's really sad to see how she keeps treating her PhD students, and not the least the women, but what am I supposed to do? I'm just one of them, with no power, and anyhow I have to think about my own situation, because if I defend them I will get into trouble myself. It's not so easy, you know, if I don't put myself first, no one else does.

> We sat in the office of the head of department, and she told her version and then I was supposed to tell my version, but even as I spoke I felt the doubt growing in the room, even in myself—is this really how it happened, or had I misunderstood everything? Was this in fact just a "version," as the chair put it, or was it the real thing? In the end, I didn't file a complaint

© INGELA NILSSON, 2022 | DOI:10.1163/9789004521025_002

because the whole situation made me feel so insecure and I had no witness to either the "incident" or the meeting. There are so many guidelines, rules and even laws, but somehow they rarely seem to work in practice.

It's not as if he did anything, I mean nothing sexual, he didn't touch me or anything, never. It was just the way in which he talked about women, always bringing up sexual situations from novels or films or the real world. The framed poster he had in his office, depicting half-naked women in some sort of ancient setting. The way in which he would always stand too close to you, forcing you to raise you head in order to look him in the eyes. The handwritten notes he would leave in your pigeon hole, instead of sending an email. Or even emails that were somehow too private, but never crossing the line. But he never did anything, of course, it's not as if it was harassment, it was just super uncomfortable. But that's life, you know, all these men acting more or less correctly in the open but secretly waving their dicks. What can you do?

So I said, "This is not OK, you were so mean to him, this is no way to behave, you should apologize." But even though they had all heard what had been said and had seen the student fighting back his tears at the comments of the senior professor and then leave the room crying, no one wanted to support my complaint. The student was inexperienced and spoke broken English, the professor was a large man with a red face and a loud voice, knowing how to exert his power. They all knew that if they objected to his behavior, they might be next. My written complaint was countered by a letter from the dean, explaining that this is "simply the way he is," nothing to be upset about.

Everyone knew about his right-wing ideas, of course, they were no secret and when he invited people over for drinks he was rather outspoken. But, I mean, it was his house and it's a free country, right? Of course, that last event was unpleasant and people obviously got very upset, the Nazi thing might have been too much. But still, telling the whole story to the dean and then forcing him to apologize in public like that, it was pretty harsh, considering what a beloved teacher he had been for so long. What was the point, really, what did she gain by turning him in? Anyhow, it was all forgotten after that and things went back to normal, he kept teaching for at least ten more years and was awarded a pedagogical prize. We all make mistakes you know, we're just people.

I agree he's a bit creepy, that's no secret, but it's your responsibility to handle him. Make sure you dress decently, button up your shirt properly—not like today—and don't wear short skirts. Don't provoke him and he probably won't do anything to you. This is the way it is, so you might as well get used to it, that's what I did, it's what we all do.

Then she went on and on about all the important places she'd been to and the important people she'd met and knew, and how much they appreciated her, and I really tried to look interested because after all she is my senior and my supervisor, but in the end I felt that I had to say something, so I waited for her to take a breath and then I cut in, telling her that my article had been accepted by that journal. I expected her to be pleased, since she had read it and actually been quite helpful, but she looked at me as if I had offended her, then forced a smile and said "congratulations." She then turned to her desk, shuffled around some papers and told me that our meeting was over, she had important things to do.

I was at the point of crying and then someone at the back of the room stood up and said, "Enough now, let's move on. But first a five-minute break." It was a professor I had never met before, from a different university, and as I was smoking a cigarette during the break, still fighting back my tears, he came up to me. At first he said nothing, just lit his cigarette and stood there, smoking. Then he said, "Sometimes people still do that to me, try to make me feel small, intimidating me in front of others. But then I imagine them as tiny people with tiny voices, of little or no importance. Let them whimper." He put out his cigarette, nodded to me and left.

I have tried putting the voices in the freezer, but they come back and haunt me, sitting on the kitchen shelves, whispering from behind the bathroom mirror, sometimes sitting at the breakfast table while my partner and I have our eggs. I make up a Linnaean system in my head: Helplessness, Power abuse, Boundaries ... Why so few stories in the categories of Respect, Integrity, Solidarity? There must be more such stories, I'm sure there are more, but right now I just need to find space to store them. Not in my head, but perhaps in a book. Yes, a book might be a good idea. Taking us from despair to hope. Yes, a book, they all have to go into a book.

© MONICA HELLSTRÖM, 2022

CHAPTER 3

What My CV Doesn't Tell You

Julie Hansen

> A good CV showcases your skills and your academic and profes-
> sional achievements concisely and effectively. It's well-organized
> and easy to read while accurately representing your highest accom-
> plishments.
>
> "WRITING AN EFFECTIVE ACADEMIC CV" (2019)

∴

The academic *curriculum vitae* is a special genre, designed to be both terse
and exhaustive, plodding a straight and narrow path of *education, employment,
publications* ... At the same time, it is selective, trumpeting high points only,
never lows. Unexplained gaps would hint vaguely of failure.

A recent application for something or other prompted me to undertake the
tedious task of updating my CV. As I added new entries, I began to reflect on
the kinds of professional experience, often unsought and painfully gained, that
a CV will never acknowledge. To fill in those blanks requires a less self-assured
genre, one that allows for the winding implied by the literal meaning of *curriculum vitae*—"course of life." What follows is my attempt at an alternative CV.

In her memoir *Educated* (2018), Tara Westover relates what it was like to
study at Cambridge University in the new millennium. In the popular imagination, an arrival at Cambridge signals success, and so it is in the narrative arc
of Westover's story:

> After the porter left I stood, bookended by my suitcases, and stared out my
> little window at the mythic stone gate and its otherworldly battlements.
> Cambridge was just as I remembered: ancient, beautiful. I was different.
> I was not a visitor, not a guest. I was a member of the university. (p. 255)

She tells of an unusual upbringing in rural Idaho, with survivalist parents who
were prepping for Armageddon and kept their children out of school. Against
these odds, the self-taught Westover manages to get a higher education, earning

a PhD in history. To Westover, education represents freedom and self-invention, yet when she arrives at Cambridge, she feels out of place.

The circumstances of my own entry into academia fall somewhere between Westover's and those of the other students she describes as blending in seamlessly at Cambridge. After graduating from high school, I enrolled at the state university on the other side of the lake. The oldest things on campus were trees, but I entered its halls (Collegiate Gothic style, anno 1950) with a sense of awe not unlike Westover's at Cambridge. True to its etymology, the place served up the universe from an infinitude of perspectives. I was drawn to study literature for its capacity to explore the full range of human experience through words alone.

As an undergrad, I had only the vaguest awareness that there could be a backside to this world that so entranced me. Not until later did I realize there is no direct correlation between intellectual refinement and treating others well. There were occasional rumors of misconduct, but I didn't want to hear these stories, much less believe them. I told myself they were anomalies in an otherwise benign world. Decades later, my former undergraduate advisor and longtime mentor would relate over dinner some scandals from the era of my student days. I didn't want to hear them then either, and my conflicted reaction sparked our first disagreement in years (but I'm getting ahead of myself here ...).

Looking back, I imagine that my aunt, the black sheep of the family and the only other one to earn a PhD, must have faced obstacles as a professor in the 1970s. When I was a teenager, she made me promise never to learn to speed type, on the logic that people can't treat you like a secretary if you don't have secretarial skills. I broke this promise, naively secure in the belief that, after the battles fought by her generation, I would never encounter sexism in my chosen career.

My undergraduate degree was made possible by a combination of scholarships, student loans and the modest help my parents could provide. High tuition made graduate school a long shot, but thanks to a fellowship from a prestigious university, I could afford to spend a few more years studying literature. It was in grad school that the contours of the downside of academic life began to sharpen. The graduate students tiptoed around a temperamental departmental secretary, lest she wield her informal power to our disadvantage. Every Tuesday and Thursday at 3 pm, my small cohort would breathe a collective sigh of relief at having made it through another seminar on medieval literature without freezing up or starting to cry. Misery loves company, but even this kind of camaraderie can crack and fissure. In the beginning we were four, then three—too few to withstand the atmospheric pressure. In an unforgiving environment, it becomes harder to forgive one another.

Some professors exchanged harsh words in the corridors, others didn't speak at all. The majority were nice to students, but one seemed to take out aggression obliquely, on the graduate students supervised by a colleague he disliked. It was this that reduced me to tears at my oral exams. Afterwards I was mortified not so much by the belittling words, as by my own show of weakness in response. Many times since in my academic career, I've told myself I need to toughen up.

Another graduate student consoled me with the fact that no one in recent departmental history had passed their orals without breaking down. To the credit of the compassionate department chair, I received her apology the next day. She was not present at my exams, but had heard. Somehow, everyone had. She called the incident unforgivable and attributed it to a feud that had nothing to do with me. It helped to hear this, and I had, after all, passed with distinction. You've been vindicated, said my consoler. Yet that moment of undeserved humiliation influences how I approach exam situations to this day. Some colleagues might think I'm too quick to intervene on behalf of students, but I can't tell students to toughen up, seeing as that's never worked for me.

At the same time, the intense experience of graduate school was addictive. Never have I learned so much in so little time (even from the one professor who was not so kind). I basked in the aura of brilliant minds. The faculty were generous with their time and knowledge, my dissertation advisor ever-patient and encouraging. A slow reader, I lived by necessity with my nose in a book, spending entire contented days in an overstuffed armchair in the graduate reading room (Art Deco, anno 1938). I made my way through long reading lists, transformed by what I consumed. I traveled to my first conferences and took summer research sojourns in Europe. Two Nobel laureates gave poetry readings at my department. I was acquiring a taste for the intellectual pleasures of this profession, and there was no question that the good outweighed the bad.

Not long after defending my dissertation, I got lucky on the job market and accepted a position in a department distinguished by a collaborative spirit. As a product of the American educational system transplanted to Europe, I had a steep learning curve to climb, but my colleagues gave me a leg up. It was from them that I really began to learn how to teach.

I was fortunate to come to such a welcoming department straight out of grad school, but I've since witnessed disasters in the academic workplace. I've seen a thriving department, overflowing with students, decimated by internal strife that no one could get a handle on. The solution in the end was to downsize, rendering half the faculty redundant. Before we reached that sorry state, however, there was a five-day group therapy retreat, led by a consultant in Birkenstocks with a mandate to diagnose and treat our deficiencies. We sat in a circle eight hours each day, urged to reveal our innermost thoughts and feelings. "There will be yin and yang, crying and screaming," the therapist had (rather alarmingly) explained to me over the phone when I tried (unsuccessfully) to get myself excused on the grounds that I was eight months pregnant. He assigned us divisive little tasks, like listing the five best and worst traits of each colleague. Reluctance to participate was viewed as an act of insubordination, of which there were plenty over the course of the retreat. If any good came of that experience, it was that it united us in collective distaste and resistance. On the fourth day, the therapist lost patience and accused us of undermining his work. "Never in twenty years," he complained, "have I met such a hopeless group of people."

Once an organizational psychologist, who had been hired by a university to investigate a harassment complaint, explained what he thought I needed to know: that being undermined by colleagues is a normal part of any workplace—the implication being that I should just toughen up. Needless to say, I haven't followed this advice, and it turns out that part of my education has entailed learning what I am no longer willing to accept.

Yet my worklife has been far from bad—consult my CV and you will see the high points. I have been the beneficiary of generous resources, monetary as well as less quantifiable kinds, such as encouragement, kindness and constructive feedback. I have experienced the deep satisfaction that comes from collaboration with colleagues on equal terms, unmarred by envy and competition. And the classroom always provides a welcome refuge from collegial strife.

The truth of the matter is that the course of my academic life has wound through both good and bad, and as time goes on, it's getting harder to reconcile the two. Once, when intradepartmental intrigues got so bad as to make me ill, the physician who examined me asked where I worked. On hearing the answer, she shook her head knowingly, making it clear I was not the first from my profession to turn up in her clinic. Yet I continue along the well-trodden path, still hoping the good can be made to outweigh the bad.

The above-mentioned dinner with my mentor took place at a critical juncture in my professional life. By outward measures, things could hardly have been going better, but I had been suffering at an unhappy department for months and inwardly knew the situation was untenable. Between the main course and dessert, my mentor inquired if things had improved. They had not, I explained. My mentor raised an eyebrow, expressed sympathy and offered some well-intentioned but disappointing advice. *Don't fight back, it will only make things worse.* And it was then that the revelations poured forth about professors I had admired as a student. In a childlike reflex, I wanted to cover my ears to keep from hearing things I would rather not know. At the same time, an angry question formed on my lips. *Why are you telling me this only now?* My appetite for dessert was gone, replaced by a sense of betrayal. He said he hadn't wanted to discourage me from pursuing an academic career, that he had hoped things would get better over time.

A few days later, my mentor sent an apologetic note and I forgave, knowing that the problem is a joint inheritance. He had just retired after a long and significant career, and now I was the one in a position to dispense advice. His choice back then was now mine to make—of what to be silent, and of what to speak. This book is part of my choice.

References

Westover, T. (2018). *Educated: A memoir*. Random House.

Writing an effective academic CV. (2019). Elsevier. https://www.elsevier.com/connect/writing-an-effective-academic-cv

CHAPTER 4

Notes from the Margins of Academic Life

Anonymous 1

1   Academic Harassment

> They say, we've never seen him behave like that, so you must be lying.
> (Chanel Miller, *Know My Name*)

Dear Madam Chair,

Thank you for agreeing to see me and for agreeing with yourself throughout our protracted and unpleasant interview. It was indeed consoling to learn that I have imagined the whole unhappy affair; now I can make an appointment with my doctor and ask for a referral to the psychiatric services. Your confirmation that Dr. X. has never bullied you was particularly reassuring; had he raped me, the fact that he has not once raped you would certainly serve as a very useful witness statement in his defense.

Permit me to congratulate you on your tactics. Pretending total ignorance of the circumstances was a masterstroke (although, for future reference, it might have been more effective to have maintained the pretense consistently throughout). I shall always be indebted to you for your invaluable advice, applicable to so many difficult professional situations. Above all, I will remember the golden maxim that when two people have a conversation behind closed doors, either one of them is free to deny anything that was said afterwards. In this context, I am assuming that your belittling and patronizing comments would, if repeated by me, be added to the list of things I have imagined.

Finally, I would like to thank you for pointing out to me how grateful I should be for the privilege of being associated, albeit in the remotest possible sense, with the Faculty, and for clarifying my position in the University as an official non person. I shall take care to refer to myself in future as "non persona non grata," a title that does honor not just to me but to the wider academic community.

Yours etc., etc.

© JULIE HANSEN AND INGELA NILSSON, 2022 | DOI:10.1163/9789004521025_004

2   Academic Collaboration

One of my greatest research pleasures has always been collaborative projects. My first was with two other women. We investigated the presentation of men and women, from literary and social perspectives, in a medieval poem. Afterwards, I heard myself referred to at a conference as "one of those three weird lesbians." (Why else would women want to work together?) I have to admit that in persisting, and going on to publish with one of my fellow-"lesbians" a paper on Renaissance love poetry, I was asking for trouble. (Isn't that what women do?)

My next two collaborative research ventures happened to be with a man. This did not improve matters. First of all, the editor assumed we were a couple and sent a single set of proofs to my home address. I had to photocopy them and mail them, as my supposed "partner," far from living in my marital home (which might have come as some surprise to my husband, especially after the "lesbian" revelation) was in another country. After our second joint publication, my head of department at the university (a woman) called me in for some career advice. I was to cease and desist from research collaboration with a man, because everybody would assume that the results were all his own work; none of mine. (Really?)

Over the years, I have gone from bad to worse, collaborating with people who self-identify in various ways. One thing they have in common, though, is that they do not use gender or sexual identity as insults or even grounds for suspicion.

Note to the Reader: Please don't imagine that you have to sleep with your research collaborators. You can, if you like, of course. As it happens, I didn't.

3   Academic Milestones

> When I was just eighteen,
> You interviewed me for a place at university.
> You said, "The boys will all run after you;
> How will you cope?"

> When I was twenty-eight,
> You offered me advice before an academic interview.
> You said, "Just smile your charming smile."

> When I was thirty-eight and just-divorced,
> You crept up on me and kissed my neck.
> Your wife was in the next room.

When I was forty-eight,
You started telling colleagues I was "difficult."

When I was fifty-eight,
You went too far.
I called you out,
and now, Sir, out you are.

So when I tell my students about teachers who inspired me,
Oddly enough, I never mention you.

Publisher's Note

The author's identity is anonymized for this chapter. Brill is aware of the real identity of the author. The inclusion of anonymized chapters has been permitted by Brill in view of risks to the general security of the author.

CHAPTER 5

A Decisive Meeting in Department X

Dinah Wouters, Tim Noens, Thomas Velle and Anonymous 2

1   Email Invitation

From: Frank Jacobs <frank.jacobs@university.edu>
Date: Friday, April 20, 2020 at 11:51 AM
Subject: Convening an extra meeting of the departmental committee
To: Department list

To all members of the Department of X
To all members of the Department Council

Dear Colleagues,

Today, the Faculty Board has forwarded the request by the Chancellor and the co-directors, addressed to all departments, to draw up a report in view of the general well-being of their members, teaching staff, research fellows, administrators and students. Our particular attention is asked for the situation of the doctoral students and the postdoctoral fellows, due to some recent commotion in the press. You all know the background and it would be useless to come back to the case itself, but, nonetheless, we will have to take a position on what was transmitted to the press and mainly on how to avoid similar things from happening in our department. This report will constitute one of the preparatory documents to be handed over to those responsible for the risk analysis that our department will be subjected to as a result of the recent events. As this risk analysis ought to start before the end of this month, we are obliged to convene a department meeting at the beginning of next week. Our meeting is planned for Monday, and we start early, at 10 am, because we need a true discussion in order to have a first draft of the report.

   Both by email and during a quick and improvised discussion, a number of colleagues have tried to single out some of the more urgent points and problems in view of the risk analysis. They particularly paid attention to the difficulties PhD students encounter in their relationship with their supervisors. They could take as a basis the recent PhD survey as it was conducted among

© DINAH WOUTERS ET AL., 2022 | DOI:10.1163/9789004521025_005

PhD students of the entire university and of our faculty. I am very grateful for this work done by Prof. Susan Haas, Prof. Paul Renard and Prof. Olivia Monti.

In the end, they came up with following points that we must take into consideration:

- How do we welcome junior members in the department?
- How do we inform junior members about what is expected from them?
- How do we stimulate junior members to talk about problems if they ever encounter them?
- How can we help junior members find the resources that are designed to help them?

Although we think it superfluous to stress, we still want to emphasize that the meeting is not meant to address the concrete event in which our near colleague is involved nor the commotion it caused in the press. We can assure all members of the department that the university authorities are taking care of this. Our only task is to ask how our department fulfills its responsibilities in the future as to the guidance of PhD students and postdoctoral research fellows. We hope to draft the most essential elements of the report as we must transmit it to the committee that was entrusted with screening our department.

With kind regards,
Frank Jacobs

2 Meeting

F. Jacobs: Thank you all for coming today, I know you are all very busy. Unfortunately, it came to my attention only after the invitation was sent that there is an overlap between this department meeting and the Career Day for early-career researchers organized by the university. I regret that, but I thought it would be better not to bother you all with additional emails and new dates. And we are in a hurry, as we mentioned. I can see there aren't that many PhD students and postdocs present today, but I'm sure the other participants will be able to empathize with their position and voice their concerns. We've all been there, haven't we?

O. Monti: It's not illogical that we as academic staff have a somewhat stronger representation in meetings. Anyway, there is a nice balance between men and women today, that's good at least.

F. Jacobs: Given the subject of the meeting, I would have preferred to see more PhD students. But I can assure everyone that we will take this matter with us to the preparation of the next meeting. Before we start, we just have to deal with a small problem. Our secretary has been ill since yesterday, so I'm looking for a volunteer to take notes. Any candidates? Perhaps one of the PhD students?

S. Nielsen: Ehm, yes, I could do that.

F. Jacobs: That's wonderful. Thank you so much, Sander. You can start off by noting the names of the people present. Full professors, let's see ... Susan Haas, Olivia Monti, Paul Renard ... and Ian Lang. Do I forget anyone? Emma Davies, then, is assistant professor, as well as Lucia Flores. And the doctoral students present are ...

S. Eder: Sara. Sara Eder.

F. Jacobs: Sara, right. So, Sara Eder and yourself, Sander. I don't see Nicolas here. And Emily is also absent, you might have to note that as well.

S. Nielsen: So, there are no postdoctoral researchers present?

F. Jacobs: I'm afraid not, Sander. I'll first give the word to Emma, our ombudsperson, who will talk you through the results of the PhD survey. She won't say anything about the unfortunate case that has recently occurred between the colleague from our department and one of his PhD students. As I wrote in my email, we all regret what happened but we have to get past this specific case. The aim of this meeting is to look towards the future. Emma, the floor is yours.

E. Davies: Thank you, Frank! I'll keep it short. In the survey, PhD students were asked for their opinion about various aspects of the department's doctoral guidance policy. Two results are relevant within the context of this meeting. The first concerns the guidance PhD students receive from their supervisor. The second is about the conflicts PhD students have already experienced with their supervisor. We're talking here about serious and long-running conflicts about matters like intellectual property, abuse of power, sexual or other kinds of intimidation, racism and discrimination, and so on. You can see both results projected on the screen.

S. Haas: Thank you, Emma. I must say that I am very happy with these results. Seventy percent of the PhD students are satisfied with the guidance by their supervisor: a clear majority!

P. Renard: And only fifteen percent claim to have already had a more serious conflict with their supervisor. It is such a relief to read that. The newspapers from the past few days, reporting on the unfortunate recent case, gave the impression that this department is full of predators who routinely mistreat their PhD students. This result clearly shows that these kinds of conflicts are just exceptions.

F. Jacobs: The press communication has been very difficult. It has been impossible for me as the department's chair to gain control over the story. Before you have a chance to speak up, journalists have twisted your words and written all sorts of things about our department that are simply not true.

I. Lang: You did a good job, Frank. And as Paul and Susan said: the results of the survey prove that our efforts are widely appreciated by our PhD students. Let's focus on these numbers and not on what the press has been saying about us.

S. Eder: With all respect, but I find it difficult to follow your interpretations of the survey's results. These numbers also mean that more than 1 in 4 indicate that they receive insufficient guidance. And I don't think that fifteen percent reporting on serious conflicts is insignificant. On the contrary!

I. Lang: You are right, Sara. But we should also look at the response rate, of course, which is 37 percent. I suspect an overrepresentation of people who are unsatisfied or have some personal grievance with their supervisor. In that case, 30 and 15 percent is really not that much. You cannot make everyone happy. Some people just fill out these surveys to get back at someone.

S. Eder: Can I say something to that? I don't want to deny that resentment might play a minor role, but if we assume that the survey is not representative, why do we take it as the basis for this discussion?

S. Nielsen: I do think it gives a good picture of the fact that the majority of people have no complaints and have developed a good relationship with their supervisor. Of course I agree with you, Sara, that we should reach out to these few exceptions that are experiencing problems.

S. Haas: But how can we reach out to them? The survey is anonymous. If they do not come to the ombudspersons of their own accord, what can we do?

O. Monti: It's such a shame that people use these surveys to complain but do not come to us with their problems. We cannot do anything if they don't take the first step.

L. Flores: That's easy to say, but from what I hear from my own PhD students, people find it hard to take that step and report problems they are facing with their supervisor. The low response might also be an indication of this, even though the survey was anonymous. PhD students are dependent on their supervisor for guidance, a network, and recommendations in the future. We should not underestimate this.

P. Renard: I would be very sad to hear that PhD students do not trust the good-will of their supervisors. All people make mistakes, of course, and academics are very busy people, but I cannot think of anyone in this department who does not take the well-being of his students to heart.

O. Monti: or her—

P. Renard: Beg your pardon?

O. Monti: Or her. You said "his students"—

P. Renard: Right, of course.

L. Flores: Perhaps you should say that to the PhD student who was sexually assaulted by one of our colleagues last week, Paul.

P. Renard: That's a very unfortunate case!

L. Flores: That we as a department allowed to happen!

F. Jacobs: Let's not get emotional! I see your point, Lucia. Actually, Emma and I anticipated it. Right, Emma?

E. Davies: Yes! Frank asked me to develop a concrete plan to prevent similar cases in the future and to optimize the department's doctoral policy. First of all, I wrote a protocol listing a couple of good practices regarding doctoral guidance. We can hand this document to new PhD students. In this way, it will be immediately clear to them what the department expects of them and what they may expect of their supervisor.

P. Renard: You said "protocol." Does this mean this will be a binding instrument?

E. Davies: Well, yes. From my experience as the ombudsperson, I can say that it's better to have clear rules. But I can assure you that all the guidelines I propose are very reasonable. I state, for instance, that supervisors must talk with their PhD students about their research on a regular basis, at least once per trimester. I also include a paragraph on how to give feedback in a decent way, and another one on respecting each other's professional and personal boundaries.

O. Monti: Aren't we overreacting? Just because there are a handful of troubled relationships between a PhD student and a supervisor in the department, we do not suddenly need moral protocols. I don't see why we should hold everybody to the same little rules because of a few cases where things go wrong.

P. Renard: I mean, where are we, kindergarten? We are all highly intelligent people who should be trusted with knowing what works best for us.

L. Flores: What strikes me is that the discussion has so far been dominated by professors. Correct me if I am wrong, but I think I am attending a meeting on the well-being of PhD students. So perhaps we should listen to what they have to say. Sander, I see you are busy writing, but what is your opinion on the measures that have been proposed?

F. Jacobs: Good point, Lucia! Please, Sander, speak up!—

S. Nielsen: Well, ehm, it is clear that it is a complex debate. I have a good relationship with my supervisor—

O. Monti: Thank you, my dear. I also think that we have an excellent connection—

S. Nielsen: Regardless, I think it will be good to have a protocol on PhD guidance. As PhD representatives, we have been asking for such a document for a long time. Also, I agree with Emma that the protocol should be more than a list of good practices. It should be an instrument for PhD students to hold their supervisors accountable. I mean, in case of lacking guidance or abuse of power, where it is really necessary. In my case, for instance, there is no need.

I. Lang: "Accountable?" This horrifies me. What has become of mutual trust and respect? Only people who cannot take responsibility for their own problems would call in the help of protocols, accountability, rules. It horrifies me that the university is turning more and more into a place where everyone mistrusts each other and we must account for everything that we do.

S. Nielsen: That is not what I mean. I am as wary as you are of the corporatization of universities, but I am not calling for more optimization or administrative burdens. On the contrary, I want more responsibility in dealing with each other.

I. Lang: Exactly, responsibility. That includes the responsibility of supervisors to provide guidance and the responsibility of PhD students to stand up for themselves. If I think about how it used to be ... in our time, we were not waiting for others to come and ask us how we were doing. We had to stand up for ourselves!

F. Jacobs: Please let us stay calm. We can decide whether or not we make these guidelines a binding instrument in a later meeting. Incidentally, the issue of taking responsibility to come forward with complaints brings us seamlessly to the next point, right, Emma?

E. Davies: Indeed. Apart from the protocol, we need to think about ways to encourage PhD students to talk about their problems. As the ombudsperson, I was shocked that I wasn't aware of the misbehavior from one of our colleagues, until I read about it in last week's newspapers. How can we find out about these issues more quickly? How can we help these PhD students?

O. Monti: You shouldn't blame yourself, Emma. You are a wonderful ombudsperson. Really.

I. Lang: Absolutely! You can't help it if PhD students don't come to you.

E. Davies: I know. But how can I make them come to me?

F. Jacobs: Any ideas?

P. Renard: Well, our department's website really is a mess. Everything is so unclear there. It wouldn't surprise me if PhD students who want to ask for help simply get lost.

E. Davies: So, you suggest improving the website?

P. Renard: Yes! But this will probably take a while. For now, we can place this information on the home page.

F. Jacobs: Excellent idea, Paul. That should help! I'll pass this to the website's administrator. Sander, have you written down this suggestion? It should go into the meeting's minutes. I shall also mention it in the press release that I have to send out this evening, together with the protocol Emma proposed. Any other suggestions?

S. Eder: I don't have the feeling that we are taking this serious enough. The case that elicited this meeting is very serious and the media do have a point when they talk of widespread abuse of power. [Indignant exclamations, Sara speaks louder.] I heard you talking about responsibility and trust. I am talking about people in power not taking their responsibilities and people in precarious positions not being able to trust those in charge. This case is not an exception, and it rests on many smaller abuses that pass unreprimanded each day.

F. Jacobs: Alright, Sara, general accusations are not very helpful. Can you give us a few examples of what you are referring to?

S. Eder: I am referring to supervisors who will not grant their PhD students the right to a holiday, who expect them to be at their beck and call at all times, who invade their personal space, who appropriate their publications through unrightful co-authorship, or who do not provide any guidance at all.

I. Lang: If these problems are as omnipresent as you say, why do we hear nothing about this? Examples are all very well, but can you give us names? Why are these people not speaking to us?

S. Eder: I hear from many of my colleagues that taking this first step is difficult because they haven't met any examples in their surroundings of problems that have been properly solved by taking such a step. It's the reigning impunity and a certain powerlessness of the administrative course they have to take that makes it not worthwhile to even start with it.

F. Jacobs: I'm not sure what you are insinuating.

E. Davies: Indeed, as the ombudsperson, I sometimes feel quite powerless myself when I cannot help a situation move forward. I'm not allowed, for example, to get back in touch with someone who had been complaining about a malpractice before. The initiative should always come from this person.

F. Jacobs: Yes, but that is for privacy reasons, of course. It is not our responsibility or even within our powers to look back, I'm afraid.

L. Flores: But it is there you find the malpractices! You should not interview current PhD students, but PhD students who have left, who have not finished their PhDs, etc.

S. Haas: That, I find, is very dangerous. They are full of grievances towards their old job. Did you know, by the way, that the word "ombudsman" goes back to the Old Norse umboðsmaðr, which means representative? You can only represent someone who wants to be represented.

[Hesitant silence.]

S. Eder: The problem is that our jobs are temporary and that our future in academia depends on the recommendations of our supervisors. And we should not forget another characteristic of our academic culture: most of the PhD students are very young, often doing a PhD as their first experience with a working environment. How would they know what is normal and abnormal, also in a working environment that is loosely structured in comparison with other sectors?

F. Jacobs: That's why agreeing on good and bad practices is important. We should communicate them more clearly to the PhD students when they start, so they know their rights.

S. Eder: I just wanted to explain why most people don't even take the first step. Once they know something is not right, they are probably closer to the finish than to the start of their PhD, so why risk the entire endeavor at that point? Why would they even come to a department meeting discussing matters that will be implemented long after they are gone, in the best-case scenario?

S. Haas: It seems as if you are implying that all professors are bad guys who intimidate and bully their PhD students. 70 percent are satisfied with the guidance they receive from their supervisor. 70 percent!

F. Jacobs: Let's all stay calm. Perhaps that's also good advice in case of conflicts. Stay calm, talk to each other and eat cake together. In my experience, a freshly baked cake can do wonders.

O. Monti: Absolutely! Almond cake is my personal favorite, I admit.

F. Jacobs: Good choice, Olivia! All kidding aside, I take note of your concerns, Sara, thank you for your intervention. For now, we stick to the plan to communicate the protocol. If necessary, we can take extra measures.

E. Davies: In my experience, it is often the little things that help create a good and inviting environment. The other day, we went with a group of colleagues to a bar, which was very nice.

F. Jacobs: Of course, not all supervisors should have to go to a bar with their students. Personally, I think one should also keep a certain distance.

E. Davies: Perhaps it is a good idea to work with large pieces of paper to make mood boards in smaller groups, to brainstorm together and work out some suggestions to improve the work environment.

S. Haas: Maybe that suggestion should be tabled until the next meeting. That deserves a separate get-together.

F. Jacobs: Indeed, Susan, that might be a good idea, but let me remind you all that we have been making quite some progress already. Olivia already took the initiative earlier this year to have a group sport activity. The turnout was quite poor, but we might have to make this into an annual activity, every year another sport or an excursion.

[Person in the back coughs.]

F. Jacobs: We are also currently having discussions with the university about the possibility of moving some things around in the building in order to create space for new breakrooms.

[Happy chatting.]

F. Jacobs: An update on this will be given later this month. We will also reconsider coffee machines. We had those in the past, but the machines tended to break down and the repair costs turned out to be too high. But as I hear you all speak today, I will move this up on the priority list. I will also contact some people to create a team to organize these annual team building activities ...

L. Flores: [muttering indistinctly] Ridiculous ...

[Lucia Flores leaves the room; door slamming.]

F. Jacobs: I see some colleagues are leaving; we are indeed running overtime. I want to thank everyone for their engagement. I think this meeting has been very fruitful, given the short time. I will end by briefly summarizing the measures we have agreed upon: first, to put together a list of good practices concerning the guidance of PhD students, second, to put the necessary information for PhD students, like the ombuds and health services, more visibly on the faculty website, and third, to organize yearly team-building activities. Sander, will you communicate these measures to the doctoral and postdoctoral researchers and put them in the minutes? Thank you so much. I have to run now. Take care!

Minutes of the meeting

Meeting of the departmental committee in response to the request by the Vice-Chancellor to carry out a risk analysis and propose some measures towards improving the well-being of doctoral students and postdoctoral employees

Date and time: Monday, April 23, 2020, 10:00-12:00

Present:
Professor Frank Jacobs, head of department
Professor Susan Haas
Professor Olivia Monti
Professor Paul Renard
Professor Ian Lang
Professor Emma Davies
Assistant Professor Lucia Flores
Sander Nielsen, doctoral student
Sara Eder, doctoral student

Absent:
Dr. Emily Smith, postdoctoral researcher
Nicolas Leroy, doctoral student

Chair: Professor Frank Jacobs

Minutes secretary: Sander Nielsen

Purpose of the meeting: to discuss the results of the survey and decide on measures that are needed to further the well-being of PhD students in our department

Items on the agenda:

1. Discussion of the recent survey of doctoral students
    The overall impression is positive: a majority of respondents are satisfied with the guidance they receive.
    There is concern for a minority of people who indicate that they receive insufficient guidance. The committee members hope these people will find their way to the ombudspersons.

2. How can the quality of PhD supervision be optimized?
    Action item: The ombudsperson has put together a list of good and bad practices. These will be communicated to doctoral students.

3. How can we encourage PhD students to seek help when they experience problems with their supervisor or others?
    Action item: We will bring together information on the ombudspersons and other facilities on the department's homepage.
    Next step: Create a dedicated page when the new website is launched.

4. What can we do to alleviate stress among PhD students?
    Action item: We will reconsider the costs of repair for the coffee machines, as places where people meet and connect with each other.
    Action item: We will make the excursion a yearly team-building event and advertise the event more widely.
    Next step: We will organize a meeting on the idea of mood boards that will help people to connect with each other.

3   Afterword

This contribution is fictional, although based on personal experiences and actual meetings from a group of researchers in different faculties and universities. The names and characters have been largely fictionalized.[1]

In writing this depiction, it was not our intention to address the issues concerning harassment in the workplace in a direct manner, nor to reflect on or promote certain solutions. Instead, we wanted to show the Kafkaesque situation PhD students and policymakers alike end up in, often despite good intentions. The very process that leads towards needed change in academic culture is a path scattered with surveys, meetings and reports, with half-hearted objectives, selective interim conclusions and short-term solutions. This arduous work is set in an environment that esteems intellectual freedom very highly and considers HR policies to be part of the business world, or at least to be a bit childish. Not surprisingly, individual needs and concerns hardly trickle down to the policies that are actually implemented. Accordingly, the effects on academic culture remain insignificant.

In the meantime, persons who become victims of harassment are labeled as the exception. They are either "vengeful" or "avoiding help," and are hereby silenced. Their anonymous testimonies are not taken seriously, or at best are considered shaky foundations for bold and general policies that potentially affect all supervisors. And thus, in this administrative process, victims of harassment become victims once more, now of seemingly harmful platitudes—the bad apple and the bunch, the half-empty or half-full glass of wine—that have real-life consequences and deprive them and their future colleagues of any perspective.

Above all, we wanted to show that the systemic nature of this process, most clearly visible during endless meetings, has the dangerous consequence that it nullifies all sense of urgency. Before actual change is enforced or even considered as a need, PhD students have either already left academia, accepted their situation in the hopes of pursuing an academic career, or become part of the same academic milieu that condoned previous harassment. By then, the urgency appears to have gone down, as a new generation of PhD students is still in the process of discovering how academia works, separating good from bad practices, and starting to learn how to stand up for themselves and via which channels.

Although universities and faculties can vary in degrees of transparency and goodwill, it is our hope the fictional documents above will be recognizable in their core. Once this modest goal is achieved, we can all go quietly back to work. We do have meetings to attend.

Publisher's Note

The identity of one of the authors of this chapter has been anonymized. Brill is aware of the real identity of the author. The inclusion of anonymized chapters has been permitted by Brill in view of risks to the general security of the author.

Note

1   We are very grateful to the colleagues and friends with whom we discussed this contribution and whose extensive suggestions and feedback tremendously improved its argument. They wholeheartedly support this book's aim and intentions yet have chosen not to be mentioned by name.

CHAPTER 6

Phantom Libraries

Unspoken Words, Untold Stories and Unwritten Texts

Moa Ekbom

There are really only three things that can ruin your life in academia: outright malice, sheer incompetence (which is worse than malice) and silence. The first two are the most startling, leaving you gasping in surprise, since it is beyond you that someone would do something like that. Silence is easy and logical— you just need to avert your eyes. Malice is strangely easier to deal with, despite being infinitely more painful. It leaves little room for ambiguity, as it is usually quite clear that the intention is to hurt and batter. This makes it easier to comprehend—it is of course awful to be hated, but you can categorize it as nastiness, and occasionally it is so egregious that you can actually report it.

Abuse through incompetence, however, is harder to pinpoint, and the perpetrator is protected by their incompetence. This kind of abuse is usually committed by those in leadership roles, by mishandling a situation—for example, a malevolent campaign against a junior colleague by a senior one. Nothing can be done about this, hence incompetence is the perfect shield. This can be painfully shocking, since it can really beggar disbelief how someone employed and paid handsomely to take responsibility can bungle it so badly. Ambiguity regarding whether there is incompetence or malicious intent brings extra pain, and an added layer of paranoia. It also undermines trust in authority and in the possibility of holding a harasser accountable.

Incompetence can also manifest itself silently, through rage-inducing sins of omission. Passive failure, by pretending something never happened, follows the law of least resistance. Inertia is something we all understand, and it can even elicit envy—imagine being able to just sit and close your eyes, and not have to fight for survival. The averting of eyes is particularly beloved by academic management, since it also has an engrained aspect of gaslighting— making someone question their perception and reasoning, since the silence indicates that nothing bad has happened, and thereby the problem is dealt with as if it never existed.

By choosing not to interfere and denying any problems, the collegially elected chairs and administration aid in portraying someone who has been inappropriately touched and stalked as a delusional brazen minx who actually wanted it badly, or the passed-over junior female colleague as a ruthless hysteric, untethered from reality, who needs to wait her turn, or the harassed grad student as a confused incompetent hussy who should never have been admitted to the program. With this framing and the decision to take no action, there is nothing the abused can do, and the non-action stasis leaves everything hanging in perpetuity. You are left in a vacuum, without breathable air, the non-action having suspended everything, and the environment has become uninhabitable—you must leave. Management has thus solved the problem by forcing out the slag, the floozy and the madwoman.

There are many things that can be done at an institutional level to improve academia, such as better labor practices with better contracts and safety nets. Academic career advancement could be made less feudal, so that you are not dependent on the goodwill of your liege lord, with transparency in hiring, especially in short-term contracts. It should be in the interest of a vice chancellor to ensure there are clear avenues for reporting harassment and holding people accountable. Yet at many universities, harassment is investigated and arbitrated within a department, and everyone who has ever worked in a department knows that no one is neutral in such situations. Enamored with the idea of collegial leadership, I hesitate to call for a more professionalized managerial stratum at universities, but I have gradually come to the conclusion that collegial leadership does not work in the most fraught departments, since it places power in the hands of people who have already established friends and foes. There are very few incentives to improve the situation; the calm of the status quo where no one is questioned or has to alter behavior is infinitely more alluring than the mess of change and examination. Despite improved labor law governance in academia, inertia is beguiling and all too easy.

I have no sweeping suggestions for solutions, since academia looks different from the perspectives of different departments, universities and countries, even if they share the same kinds of abuse and harassment. When problems arise, good leadership is essential, but rare. That colleagues have a sense of responsibility and call each other out and act, instead of averting their eyes, is also essential. This is not even a culture of fear and retribution, but a natural inclination to take the easy way out. Inertia is also connected with shrinking funding in academia, as everyone must fend for themselves as money and time disappear in cut-backs and reorganizations. Permanent positions are essential for a fair, democratic and vibrant academia, since stability is necessary in order to be a responsible and conscientious colleague.

In the magical #MeToo autumn of 2017, where change seemed possible and I finally learned that it is not okay if someone masturbates in front of you without consent (thank you, Louis CK!), the online journal *Eidolon* published an article by Donna Zuckerberg on the books that were never written and never will be, because their potential writers have been harassed, shamed or just so worn out that scholarship was not possible: "But in its shadow is a second library—at once infinite and infinitesimal—of essays, articles and books that will never be written because the people who would have written them were pushed out of the field by harassment and abuse" (2017, para. 1).

This story of lost libraries mainly concerns sexual harassment, but it can easily be expanded to include all forms of abuse in academia. Abuse that is not expressed in a sexualized manner and not specifically sexist is in many respects just as tiring and shaming as that of a sexual nature. This abuse is also practiced more visibly and openly, perhaps under the guise of supervision or scrupulousness. Specific excuses can include expressing worry about someone's aptitude for academic work, with fake concern for a specific individual's personal suitability, and exclusionary approaches such as certain information not being disseminated, with some particular person always falling off the email list.

As a classical philologist, I am of course obsessed with lost texts—all that has been lost through the ages and ravages of time, as well as the haphazardness of preservation—and I think about this ghostly library every day. It includes a text or two by me, when I was too tired, beaten and angry to produce them. The lost library should be as longed for as the (probably exaggerated) Library of Alexandria, as the dispersed books that traveled with the Byzantine princess Sophia Palaiologina to Russia, or the volumes that Ansgar and his men abandoned to the Norsemen when attacked in their missionary travels.

Texts are created from language, and this is a reminder of how hard it is to speak of abuse in academia. We all prefer exacting and precise terminology, but where stories of abuse are concerned, there are only tentative phrases, with glosses and subordinate clauses galore. Once again, the #MeToo autumn, while having devastatingly little impact, at least started to lay the foundation of a language for speaking out about and narrating abuse and harassment. The non-sexual arena is in many ways equally fraught. We are still far from having the vocabulary and narrative framework to be able to talk about this, to be capable of discussing the imbalances of power in a mutually intelligible language that encompasses the past, present and future. Translation, contextualization and interpretation is hard, especially when the one trying to tell the story is developing the language. Language cannot grow in a vacuum, when there is a refusal to listen and see. Yet the evolving language helps the abused find words for what happened. This is a delicate and precarious means of communication among the bewildered, which may remain secret for some time to come.

In all probability, I will continue to work within the same field as my harass-
ers and their passive enablers for a very long time. I will see how others support
and laud them, and how they will be given opportunities to hurt others. I can
leave, of course, and I probably should, especially if I want to leave the anger
and sadness behind. I might one day, but for now, I control my anger and grief,
and I think of the library of lost books, and how one day it will no longer be a
secret library, but a public one, where we can learn, invent and discover words,
and ensure they are correctly transmitted and interpreted.

Reference

Zuckerberg, D. (2017, December 1). The lost library: E(i)ditorial—Philomela's tapestry.
   Eidolon. https://eidolon.pub/the-lost-library-dcac1adeb281

CHAPTER 7

On the Occasion of My Retirement

Cecilia Mörner

Last winter I decided to take early retirement. For some time I had considered going down to halftime until I turned 65, which is the average retirement age in Sweden. This would have meant continuing with at least some of my duties as a lecturer for three more years. But one morning I woke up and said to myself: No! I can't! It's simply impossible. Not fulltime, not halftime, not at all. I sent off an email informing my superior and started to plan for a life with less income than I have had ever since I was a PhD student, yet with greater peace of mind than I have had for years.

What led me to make this decision, which seemed unexpected and totally illogical to most of my friends and acquaintances? I mean, as a PhD student I had struggled for years to achieve my goal of an academic job. Ever since my first position, I have shared workplaces with intelligent and exciting colleagues, and I have traveled around the world to meet other intelligent and exciting people at international conferences. My salary is good. I enjoy a high degree of independence when it comes to how I plan and carry out my lectures and seminars, and I have nice and ambitious students. I have even been offered more opportunities to do research than I have asked for. Nevertheless, I gladly leave all this behind because it will mean the end of a suffocating feeling that I believe can be traced to the occurrence of a specific phenomenon: New Public Management.

New Public Management was introduced to Swedish universities in the early 1990s in order to implement principles of the business world in the public sphere. Most notable among these were documentation, measurement, outcomes and efficiency. These keywords were, of course, established in the academic world long before New Public Management was even heard of. Academics of all times have been practicing them whenever they build research networks or decide which grade a student assignment deserves. What New Public Management brought to the table was not so much the practice of documentation, measurement, etc., but rather the *visible existence* of documentation, measurement, outcomes and efficiency. Clear instructions and templates of all kinds became mandatory. Days and hours were spent—and still are—on writing various documents intended to ensure the quality of institutions and academic work. Independent, collegial groups function as gatekeepers who guarantee that not a single wrongly spelled word or misplaced comma

© CECILIA MÖRNER, 2022 | DOI:10.1163/9789004521025_007

blemishes the syllabi. The intranet offers templates for course guides, reading lists and grading criteria in the name of efficiency and measurement. So far so good. The question is: who makes sure that all these documents are produced?

Before the introduction of New Public Management, professional administrators typed timetables and made copies of students' term papers and theses to be handed out at seminars. They did other things, too, but these were perhaps the most obvious tasks besides enrollment and registration. I worked in administration at a department for some years back then, so I know. Today, the amount of administrative tasks has grown enormously. One might expect that the vast production of documents is done by real experts with plenty of time to carry out the work. However, New Public Management focuses on the outcome of processes—not on the processes as such. It is interested in what can be documented, measured and completed in an efficient way. It requires documents which can be used to measure the outcome of a process, but what and who makes this possible are not of interest. This has resulted in a workplace culture where teachers and researchers are expected to be secretaries, though without training or even time for administrative duties.

Personally, I have no difficulty with instructions and templates. I find them timesaving. I enjoy writing course guides and I gladly publish them weeks in advance. But there is a considerable group of academics who are highly intelligent, hardworking and experienced but who do not fit into an organization which expects everybody to be their own secretary. They are the kind of academics who would have had no problem in the pre-New Public Management era, when lecturers were assumed to be eccentric and odd. In those days nobody asked for details. Timetables were posted on the wall outside the lecture hall the same day the course started, and the course books were available in the university library and the local bookstore. Nobody cared about things such as course guides. Students were concerned about the meaning of different theories, but they rarely bothered about deadlines, objectives and grades.

Today is different. In the name of New Public Management, lecturers and professors are expected to handle documents which assure students that everyone involved in a certain course can say exactly what will happen day by day and exactly what we expect from them. The actual meaning of different theories is less important than to what extent students manage to demonstrate knowledge about them. Lecturers and professors are supposed to spend as much time explaining what the students must achieve to pass with a certain grade as they do explaining the actual content of a course. Above all, lecturers and professors are supposed to know exactly where to find the kind of information students ask for. Some fail completely in this mission, a fact that results in a reality where, on the one hand, there is an incalculable amount of neatly written documents somewhere in the jungle of the intranet and, on the other hand, total chaos each time a course or a module is to be offered. The students are coming! What to do with them? They send me emails! What should I answer them? They ask which version of Bryant's book on methods they should buy! Whom am I to know? Grading criteria—what the hell is that? And what is wrong with the course guide I just posted? It is the same as last year and worked perfectly well then!

Some of my colleagues refuse to adapt to students' requirements by pointing out that it is absurd to focus on things that really do not matter in the long run. Who needs to know on which pages a certain theory was accounted for once you have graduated? Students need to understand and use theories, not remember where they read about them. I totally agree with this. Nevertheless, lectures and professors are obliged to provide visible evidence of measurement and efficiency, some of which are just for show and some of which students find intelligible. I have noticed two main strategies among my less adaptive colleagues in handling the problems, both of which often involve me. The first one is mainly used by colleagues who rarely show up at campus and work from home (even without a pandemic). They claim that they cannot log in to the intranet where the information students request can be found. They have tried several times and they have contacted university support. In vain. Could I please email them this and that document? Well, I can, and I do. It doesn't take more than five or ten minutes to find what the colleague needs. Why should I not help? However, it directs my attention away from what I *should* be doing: planning a lecture, looking for an article, writing a course guide for one of my own courses, etc. I would not mind if I were interrupted just now and then, but it happens more or less every week. Sometimes several times a day. Such days are wasted. I must either do whatever I had planned to do on a Saturday or Sunday, or give it up. The second strategy is more evasive. The colleagues who practice this strategy do not ask anything of me. Nor do they respond to students' requests. They just wait for things to happen. And things do happen. Students have their own networks and they are well-informed about the teachers. Sooner or later they will realize that the teacher in charge of their course will not answer them. Instead, they turn to me or another (usually female) teacher who has already proven willing to help. And we will patiently answer their questions and send them information about lecture halls, course literature, examinations, etc., even though it is not our responsibility. We will even revise our colleagues' outdated documents. Meanwhile, our colleagues focus on their own research projects and future lectures.

Maybe I shouldn't blame them. Who knows, perhaps they are secretly ashamed of their administrative disabilities? I know that that they have other skills that, to be honest, are as useful as the ability to write a good course guide and upload it on time. Most of them have profound knowledge about theories, methods and history, and they know everything worth knowing about various iconic researchers. But they force me into the role of a clerk because it is I and other well-organized New Public Management-adapted colleagues who compensate for their lack of administrative skills. Instead of reading a new article on a research field that interests me or drafting a research application, I found myself carrying out not only my own secretarial duties but also those of others.

You may ask why I am doing this. Why can't I just say no? I can at least tell the students that it is not my job to prepare for courses of which I am not in charge. But I do not, because I know it would cost me more energy than it does to just fix what is lacking. Students will haunt me if I do not respond to their requests. They will not be content with reading course syllabi (which are available at the external website and not too hard to find), because they are too abstract and complicated. Today's students want to know exactly which pages in a specific course book they are supposed to read and exactly how many pages they must write in the take-home exams to pass. They quickly learn the logic of New Public Management, which means that they know that some information, such as a syllabus, exists solely because it is compulsory and not because students are expected to read and understand them. Who understands the meaning of learning outcomes anyway? Syllabi are visible evidence of documentation and measurement, but they do not correspond to students' day-to-day experience of studying at a university. Students demand transparent, informative, easily digested and extremely concrete information. If this is denied them, they will make sure to denounce the course, its teachers, the program and the entire university, not only in course assessments but also on social media. Students are not just measured, they also measure. Bad student reviews will—in the name of New Public Management—be used in the overall measurement of courses and departments. And bad reviews will increase the already existing tensions within the department, where those who sacrifice their research for administrative tasks are on the verge of a nervous breakdown. I know several examples of departments that were brought down by this. Not because of a lack of academic and pedagogical skills, but because of problems with cooperation within the group due to an unfair division of labor.

I would not complain if the administrative work I do for others were compensated for in some way. Let us pretend that a colleague is working on an application for a research program while I am struggling with his or her frustrated students' questions. My colleague is aware of the favor and invites me to take part in the program. This is done with mutual respect. I know that he or she writes better applications than I do, and my colleague is aware that I am a better administrator. It is also in line with New Public Management's requirement of efficiency: those who are good at anticipating what kind of information students will request make sure that course guides, reading lists and grading criteria are available before the course starts, and those who are good at foreseeing which project will appeal to research funders write applications. Everyone would benefit from this. Unfortunately, however, this rarely happens. As a matter of fact, most of those who do not manage to write a decent course guide are not good at writing research applications either. They are good at reading hard-core theories and, to various extents, communicating their knowledge. In addition, those who are successful at writing applications usually prefer to keep their projects to themselves. They pretend not to know that administrative work is an important part of lecturers' and professors' duties, whether we like it or not. And there is absolutely nothing I can do about it.

Why not talk to your department head, you may ask. Believe me, I've tried. I have also experienced what it is like to be a department head trying to explain to lecturers and professors the importance of knowing where to find grading criteria, as well as the importance of upgrading course guides and not just copying old ones. For some employees this was not a problem. For others the request was a violation of their professionalism. I understand that. Lecturers and professors are hired for their academic knowledge and pedagogical skills, not because they are good at administration. When hiring a new faculty member, applicants' research publications are scrutinized and their ability to teach is tested. But they do not have to prove that they can foresee what students would like to know in advance. Doctoral students are trained to handle data, theories and methods, not to write course guides and answer email from students. New PhDs who get their first job as a lecturer at a university are not prepared to handle students' demands. None of us who have worked for ages were ever told how to be a good administrator. Yet, producing, finding and following instructions and manuals are indispensable skills in the New Public Management apparatus, and the job has to be done in order to make the institutional machine grind on.

The biggest injustice in this system is the fact that administrative skills do not leave any traces in one's CV. Or rather: it leaves gaps in the CV. Taking care of departmental administration and the needs of confused students does not further one's academic career. On the contrary, the more you help others by finding documents or writing new ones, the more you try to be informative, transparent and efficient when communicating with students, the less likely that you will get an article accepted in a highly rated journal or invited as a keynote speaker at an international conference. There is simply not time enough for succeeding at everything. Someone in the department will always volunteer to help his or her colleagues handle students and this person will probably do the job far more efficiently than those who have not adapted to the almost 30-year-old unspoken requirement. But in the long run, the loyal and cooperative ones are the losers. Attentive department heads may make sure to raise the hardworking lecturer-cum-administrator's salary a bit, but it does not compensate for the measly CV. The true winners are those who constantly improve their own CV by focusing on their own research and ignoring the needs of others.

However, contrary to what might appear to be my standpoint in this text, I wish that all lecturers and professors were able to concentrate on their own research and teaching. I sincerely wish that we could go back to a pre-New Public Management time when lecturers and professors focused on the meaning of knowledge and well-trained administrators took care of the administration. But finding myself squeezed between administrative demands, on the one hand, and intelligent but hopelessly dated and often selfish colleagues, on the other, was too much for me. I gave up research some years ago, and I do not mind spending all my time and energy on teaching. But I am certainly not willing to be an unacknowledged administrative slave in the academic machinery. I've had enough and I blame it on New Public Management.

CHAPTER 8

How to Be a Professor in the Twenty-First Century

Wim Verbaal

"We're heading for a time where you have intellectuals, on the one hand, and academics, on the other, and where, at the university, you will find only academics." The colleague who, about twenty years ago, addressed these words to me recently retired. At that time, we stood up together for the rights of doctoral and postdoctoral researchers. We didn't belong to the permanent academic staff. Upon his retirement, I remembered his words and repeated them to him. We had seen them come true in a frightening way.

It is no revelation that the university landscape has changed dramatically in recent decades. Nor do we lack analyses that lay bare the causes. These are usually referred to as the results of the so-called "neo-liberal policy model," based on an unrelenting belief in the forces of the market and thus in boosting "output" and generating external funds (Slaughter & Rhoades, 2000; Fleming, 2021).[1] That such a policy would prove disastrous for non-profit institutions and, within the academic landscape, for all non-industrial disciplines, seems obvious.

The former vice chancellor of a leading university in Northwestern Europe and a pivotal figure in the "neo-liberal reform" of the universities in his country once remarked that there were "too few students going in the right directions," i.e. in the technical and industrial sciences, and therefore too many going in the wrong directions, i.e. "in the humanities."[2] A look at the actual situation might reassure him: since he made his statement, enrollment in the "wrong" faculties has dropped dramatically. The neo-liberal policy model of the past decades has borne fruit. Of their own accord, people align their professional and educational choices with its objectives and, therefore, the social implications of this model can now be felt everywhere.

Of course, this has far-reaching consequences. Faculties such as those in the humanities and the arts are faced with harrowing financial cutbacks. They have to look desperately for ways to ensure their survival and, strangely enough, they mostly do so by responding precisely to the demands imposed upon them by the neoliberal policy model. The outcome is easily guessed. Whoever brings in money is rewarded. Thus, everyone starts looking for opportunities to strengthen their own position within the university institution that wants to profile itself as an academic business enterprise. Education is compromised in the first place, in spite of any protest that this is a university's most important social task. Nevertheless, university policy in general shows that whoever puts too much effort into education is punished.[3] This does not pay off, at least not immediately, and the university, like all "neo-liberal" institutions, mainly wants to generate income in the short term.

Europe offers another opportunity for those who want to make a fast career. Anyone who succeeds in obtaining European funding is welcomed with open arms by many universities and can immediately count on a permanent position, without any questions asked as to whether the scholar's specialization was necessary or an asset to the existing research or educational programs. Nor is it asked which criteria Europe applies and whether they correspond to a university's requirements of its staff. The millions in monetary resources coming in outweigh any internal policy concern (Schinkel, 2018). Researchers with little or no experience in academic education or administration will be in charge of the university for decades to come. In the meantime, absenteeism is increasing in internal councils and boards whenever they are purely policy-related and do not yield any immediate financial benefit.

Anyone who cannot knock on Europe's door or does not have the right keys to obtain European funding must secure a position in another way.[4] One such option is to become a member of those committees where money and doctoral scholarships are distributed. The past decades have seen an increase of the well-established phenomenon whereby academics manage to accumulate funds in certain councils, boards and committees while serving as a member of them. Objections are almost always countered by the statement that only the top of the research landscape is represented in such committees. However, it remains mostly unclear which criteria are used to select this elite.

Administrative positions are also limited. What can be done by those who, for whatever reason, do not qualify for similar functions? Academic funding based on output focuses on the production of articles and defended PhD dissertations. They constitute quantifiable academic production. Academics thus have to publish a great deal. They must produce an avalanche of articles. Anyone who succeeds in this is a good academic and can count on recognition with all the associated benefits. Nobody bothers about the content of such overproduction. At a meeting of my own faculty board, I heard, to my astonishment, a member of the university administration say bluntly: "It's not quality that counts. It's quantity." It should come as no surprise, then, that no questions are raised as to how an academic can find the time to produce the required quantities. And that is where the shoe really starts to hurt.

For one, plagiarism has become a significant phenomenon in academic publications. Journals, review sites and editors all have to find ways to cope with this increase of intellectual theft. And more often than before, scholars see themselves confronted with colleagues who "make use" of their results without referring to their sources. One of the main problems, however, is that plagiarists can avoid consequences once they are established names or belong to established universities, or as soon as this could mean a financial loss for their universities. The victims are mostly younger scholars who have yet to establish a scholarly reputation, or scholars employed by universities that do not belong to the select "highly rated" happy few. Rarely is the damage to their career recovered.[5] But younger scholars can fall victim to other abuses, as well.

If one browses through academic bibliographies at some universities, one might notice that a majority of publications are the work of multiple authors. The academic world seems to be an ideal world where everyone works together to achieve a beautiful joint result. Unfortunately, in many cases, the underlying reality turns out to be less rosy. Of course, fortunately many researchers work, in good conscience, together with their collaborators to achieve shared and common results and publications. But in too many cases, the truth behind such "co"-publications looks quite different. Often, the highest-ranked in the local university hierarchy simply puts their name above an article without even looking at it. The actual author suddenly sees his or her own work partly or even completely pass into the hands of someone else.

In the humanities, reference is invariably made to established practices in the applied sciences. As if there were no protest in the applied sciences against similar forms of appropriation! Internationally, criticism is growing, especially in the medical field, precisely because here these practices also extend to the work of students and interns.[6] But even apart from this, it is clear that research in the humanities is strongly based on individual commitment. Projects over long periods of time in which many researchers each carry out a small step that contributes to some far-off result are rather the exception. For this reason, any individual input must be recognized with credit given to the person who provided it. This is not only a moral obligation. It moreover avoids the violation of the right of authorship. Authorship is considered inalienable, unlike copyright (Nwabachili & Nwabachili, 2015).[7] For academics, the difference is virtually unknown, which means that, more than once, they commit intellectual theft.

Supervisors often derive their right as "co-authors" from the fact that they acquired the funds for the research. For this reason, they consider everything that is paid for by these funds to be their property. They probably envisage a parallel with what happens in industry. They do not realize, however, that, as opposed to industrial funding, they do not invest anything themselves and that the only one who can assert ownership rights is the funding association. The supervisor is no more than an intermediary who ensures that the investment (in the arts and humanities, it is usually public money) ends up with a capable researcher. For this reason, he or she cannot assert any right of ownership.

In all these cases, however, the researchers who are in one way or another involved in the publication usually act as supervisor of the actual author. But there are others who impose themselves without any official link to the author. Or who first impose a link—by making themselves co-supervisors—in order to assert themselves as "co"-authors and increase their quota of publications. Such researchers display a remarkable broadness in the specter of their expertise. They seem at home in almost all the disciplines that can be found at their home faculty. The way they manage this is by imposing themselves both on younger colleagues who are not yet adapted to modern academia and its customs and, of course, on the PhD students who feel their academic career to be under threat if they do not comply.

It is possible to go still further, for example, by appropriating the entire research of a PhD student who is subordinate to you. At international congresses, you present research as your own and under your own name, although everything you present has been collected and written by someone else to whom you refer as to "your" PhD student. Preferably, he or she should be in the room in order to answer any questions that might come up after your lecture. This way, you even display your own "generosity," because you give your students the opportunity to participate in the international debate.

Maybe you think that too risky? It is indeed easier to force the PhD student who does not want to continue, or who will in any case not secure a postdoctoral position, to leave behind all material. Now, you have ready-made texts to publish under your own name. Or you can open a page on social media for academics in the name of the student in question and upload one of the confiscated texts with your own name first. Preferably, of course, without the student knowing about it.

Does all this sound difficult to believe? Unfortunately, all these examples are drawn from real life. The victims are, of course, precisely those (post)doctoral researchers who form the unprotected middle management in many universities. They see their work published under another's name. Internationally, they lose credibility. Some obtain their doctoral degree with a dissertation based on articles that have all or largely been published with their supervisor or co-supervisor as their "co-author." To what extent can they still claim to be the author of what they have written and published?

I saw several of them succumb to the never-ending pressure to publish, as imposed on them by their (co-)supervisor wanting to meet the required quota. The pressure can become unsustainable, as can the means of imposing it. In my immediate surroundings, I have known doctoral researchers who were so severely bullied and harassed by their supervisors that they eventually needed psychiatric help. One of them is still partially incapacitated after years. Another was for three years refused even a single day off and ended up bed-ridden for a year, suffering from total burnout. Of course, such individuals are considered "unfit" for an academic career and shown the door. And the supervisors? They continue to have new victims assigned to them. For, painfully enough, many of those responsible at universities even appreciate that, in this way, doctoral researchers become accustomed to "normal" academic practice.

When addressing the question of how universities counter such practices, the answer can be as short as it is simple: nothing. University boards proudly refer to the many hotlines and committees, where complaints do indeed flow in and accumulate like litter in dead-end alleys. Nobody cleans up. If a complaint seeps through, it is "an individual case," or university boards try to erase all unpleasant traces as quickly as possible and to exonerate the scholar involved, despite the severity of the charges. Whoever dares to stand up for the victims is quickly advised to be careful in order not to be accused themselves, ending up as a prosecutor against whom charges are brought in order to annihilate the charges he himself has brought.

One could even speak of a new kind of slavery that is developing in academia. Extra money is brought in by inviting scholars from outside Western academia. The prospects of an academic career in the West are indeed still appealing for many in less prosperous countries with fewer opportunities. Those invited do not know that their invitation is often also inspired by fundraising motives. Sometimes this is a painful discovery. For, as soon as the money is received, the presence of the invited scholar is less necessary. As soon as some tension arises, he or she can simply be dismissed without further explanation. That they gave up a life in their home country, that they brought over their partner and children, that they suddenly become illegal, without work and thus without a residence permit, seems of no importance to the inviting supervisor or university. Their case now falls under the jurisdiction of the police and social services. The check has been cashed.

It is painful to realize that most of the above excesses are not limited to younger academics who are obliged to think about their careers. Established professors are guilty, yet avoid consequences. Nor is this only a gender-related problem, in which the female side always is the victim. True, women seem to suffer more, and men seem to account for the majority of bullying behavior. But one might wonder if this distribution of roles is not due more to the still predominant male part in the higher university positions. Unfortunately, women in similar positions do not always behave differently as some of the aforementioned cases show, and as became clear from some of the #MeToo discussions. As far as invited scholars from non-Western countries are concerned, the victims mostly are male.

The true problem must be looked for on a deeper level. It has to do with an incapacity to handle power over others, even in the slightest way. It has to do with loss of responsibility and respect toward the personal integrity of those who entrust themselves to your guidance and leadership.[8] But how do you check it? How can a university—supposing there is a sincere desire to prevent harassment, bullying and power abuse among staff—be sure that the individual it hires has this sense of respect and responsibility, as well as the capability to handle power?

Somehow, this is an educational problem and, of course, it is not that different from the problem hovering in the background. A society that invests all its resources in those who know how to build up their career, irrespective of the human or material consequences, will in the end create people who do not care about the safety or health of others. Perhaps universities ought to resist these developments. Perhaps universities ought to create islands of human respect and responsibility towards the other, towards the world, towards the future. Perhaps they should. But in reality, they are adapting to a system that, in the end, is destroying the true missions of the university: high-level teaching, intellectual innovation and fundamental research.

One wonders why universities do not feel the need to keep the intellectual blazon pure. That is the impression they give, anyway, but it shouldn't really come as a surprise. Unfortunately, in recent history, universities have not often been shown to excel in intellectual resistance. They rather breed academics who are obedient employees.

When my colleague, twenty years ago, made the distinction between intellectuals and academics, he didn't have all these developments in mind. But he has been proven right, perhaps more so than expected. Does this mean that there are no intellectuals left at universities? Certainly there are some. But the number is growing of those working at universities in whom the academic has gotten the better of the intellectual, in whom the craving for a career has surpassed the urge to know. And what was once called "conscience" has become extremely rare at universities. But of course, conscience has nothing to do with either career or intellect. It would merely make the university more human.

Acknowledgement

This contribution is an enlarged version of my earlier Dutch opinion piece, "Hoe word je tegenwoordig hoogleraar?"

Notes

1 On the dangerous consequences for emerging countries and economies, see Kigotho (2018). See also Runia (2018).
2 André Oosterlinck in *De Standaard*, August 25, 2011.
3 For the Netherlands, see van Oostendorp (2019); for the UK, see Graham 2015, (p. 17). For an interesting (Canadian) gendered approach to the problem of academic teaching, considered as "care work," see Fullick (2016).
4 For criticism of European Research Council policy, see Migliorato (2016) and Schneider (2017). See also Sylos-Labini (2014, 2016).
5 For just one example, see Anonymous (2017).
6 See the guidelines of ICMJE (n.d.) and COPE (n.d.).
7 See also the guidelines of US Legal (n.d.) and the EU (n.d.).
8 See Chapman (2013) and Zhao (2016). For an example, see also Hall and Betty (2020).

References

Anonymous. (2017). Plagiarism is rife in academia, so why is it rarely acknowledged? *The Guardian.* https://www.theguardian.com/higher-education-network/2017/oct/27/plagiarism-is-rife-in-academia-so-why-is-it-rarely-acknowledged

Chapman, D. (2013). Abusing power for private gain—Corruption in academe. *University World News.* https://www.universityworldnews.com/post.php?story=2013100110401544

COPE (Committee on Publishing Ethics). (2014). *What constitutes authorship?* COPE discussion document. http://publicationethics.org/files/u7141/Authorship_DiscussionDocument_0_0.pdf

EU. (n.d.). Copyright. https://europa.eu/youreurope/business/running-business/intellectual-property/copyright/index_en.htm

Fleming, P. (2021). *Dark academia: How universities die.* Pluto Press.

Fullick, M. (2016). *Changing the value of teaching in universities.* https://www.universityaffairs.ca/opinion/speculative-diction/changing-value-of-teaching-in-universities/

Graham, R. (2015). *Does teaching advance your academic career? Perspectives of promotion procedures in UK higher education.* https://www.teachingframework.com/resources/Does-teaching-advance-your-academic-career-RAEng-online-report-(April-2015).pdf.

Hall, R., & Batty, D. (2020). *'Abuse of power': should universities ban staff-student relationships?* https://www.theguardian.com/education/2020/feb/26/abuse-of-power-should-universities-ban-staff-student-relationships

ICMJE (International Committee of Medical Journal Editors). (n.d.). *Defining the role of authors and contributors.* http://www.icmje.org/recommendations/browse/roles-and-responsibilities/defining-the-role-of-authors-and-contributors.html

Kigotho, W. (2018). The dangerous rise of neo-liberal universities. *University World News*. https://www.universityworldnews.com/post.php?story=20181108130628468

Migliorato, L. (2016). *Europe's flawed race for scientific research funding.* https://undark.org/2016/09/23/european-research-council-flawed/

Nwabachili, C. C., & Nwabachili, C. O. (2015). Authorship and ownership of copyright: A critical review. *Journal of Law, Policy and Globalization, 34*.

Runia, E. (2018, January 19). Waarom ik ontslag neem bij de universiteit [Why I quit university]. *NRC*. https://www.nrc.nl/nieuws/2018/01/19/waarom-ik-ontslag-neem-bij-de-universiteit-a1589052

Schinkel, W. (2018, September 22). Waarom ik niet actievoer voor de universiteit [Why I refuse to campaign for the university]. *Groene Amsterdammer.* https://www.groene.nl/artikel/waarom-ik-niet-actievoer-voor-de-universiteit

Slaughter, S., & Rhoades, G. (2000). The neo-liberal university. *New Labor Forum, 6*, 73–79.

Sylos-Labini, F. (2014). *European science policy and research risk*. Euroscientist. https://www.euroscientist.com/european-science-policy-research-risk/

Sylos-Labini, F. (2016). *Europea: Robin Hood al contrario.* https://francescosyloslabini.info/2016/04/06/la-politica-scientifica-europea-robin-hood-al-contrario/

van Oostendorp, M. (2019). Neerlandistiek moet opkomen voor onderwijs [Dutch Studies have to defend education]. *De Nederlandse Boekengids/The Dutch Review of Books, 2*, 22–23.

US Legal. (n.d.). *Authorship in copyright.* https://copyright.uslegal.com/authorship-in-copyright/

Vasishth, S. (2017). *Lack of transparency in ERC funding decisions.* https://forbetterscience.com/2017/04/26/lack-of-transparency-in-erc-funding-decisions-by-shravan-vasishht/

Verbaal, W. (2019). Hoe word je tegenwoordig hoogleraar? *Streven, 86*, 543–547.

Zhao, Y. (2016). Vigilance of power abuse in colleges and universities. *Advances in Social Science, Education and Humanities Research, 63*, 239–243, https://download.atlantis-press.com/article/25865809.pdf

CHAPTER 9

Bad Days

Anonymous 3

It was Professor Oldboy's turn to organize the Spring School that year
But we all have bad days sometimes

Like Pedro, who, on day one, chose not to use slides
and spoke with a heavy accent
Oldboy didn't have to lecture him
on the academic courtesy of talking like a Western European

We all have bad days sometimes

Like Natalie who, on day two, took Oldboy's questions in stride
—she'd answered them when he'd nodded off
yet somehow she was made to feel stupid

We all have bad days sometimes

Professor Oldboy should have known
that the museums close early off-season,
or might, on day three, have believed Sasha, who told him so,
or he might at least have remembered her name

We all have bad days sometimes

Professor Oldboy might even, on day four, have listened
to comments I offered in the evaluation session

We all have bad days sometimes

Like the people who didn't dare to speak up
when he started shouting
his "feedback on my feedback"

And my supervisor, he might have acknowledged
the issue
when I later recounted these events
but after all, as he put it

We all have bad days sometimes

Like—all those other days—
Professor Niceguy, who calls me a nymph
after I introduce his talk
Or Eric, who persists in a third question
though I tell him we're moving on
Or Jack, who tells me he wonders
how I look in a dress
Or Andrew, who gives me the floor
because ladies go first

We all have bad days sometimes,
or is it just me?

Publisher's Note

The author's identity is anonymized for this chapter. Brill is aware of the real identity of the author. The inclusion of anonymized chapters has been permitted by Brill in view of risks to the general security of the author.

CHAPTER 10

On Diversity Workshops

Challenges and Opportunities

Hanna McGinnis, Ana C. Núñez and Anonymous 4

1 Introduction

A not uncommon occurrence within academic walls: the (usually) older white male scholar who makes an "off color" comment, or interjects a racist, sexist, classist, etc. remark into an otherwise innocuous academic presentation. Of course, for the minority targets of such opinions, these comments are not simply "off color," but rather a real aggression directed at them. Perhaps even more indicative of the lack of inclusivity and diversity in academic spaces is the fact that such toxic comments are intended as "jokes" directed at a presumed like-minded audience, the perpetrator unaware that within the room are individuals whose identities are indeed abused by such "jokes."

This was the experience of the three authors of the present article at a conference at our beloved undergraduate alma mater. In this essay, we leave the details of the not uncommon "occurrence" purposefully vague, with a shared conviction that to retell the "incident" in question would only serve to center the perpetrator yet again. To dissect the blatant personal and systemic sexism that such incidents reveal is work that has already been masterfully done by other individuals.[1]

Instead, we three current and former graduate students focus on what we accomplished in a workshop that we organized and delivered in response to such abuse of power: the labor we invested, the lessons we learned, and our hopes for greater inclusivity in those disciplines that study the pre-modern world.

In response to the inciting conference, we were approached by our trusted former undergraduate advisor to build and lead a subsequent workshop that would address, dissect and teach undergraduates about the challenges facing minority groups within graduate studies.[2] Though feeling out of our depth, we accepted the offer because we felt that by holding our own workshop to address sexism—as well as discrimination against other marginalized intersecting identities—we would transform the "incident" into a meaningful learning opportunity in which workshop participants productively worked toward greater inclusivity. Ambitions notwithstanding, we also took on this responsibility to engage with inequality in academia because we felt an obligation to not let this "incident" go unaddressed.

The workshop into which we invested four months of planning was titled: "Equity in Academia: Gender and Intersecting Identities in Graduate School, Research, and Beyond." We aimed to accomplish three things: discuss different power dynamics in academia; collectively develop a toolkit for recognizing bias; and end with a roundtable discussion with trusted faculty about their own graduate school experiences, and how, as professors, they incorporate diversity and inclusion into both their research and teaching. The workshop aimed not only to share information about biases in the academic world, but also to collectively develop and explore tools so that we can all be active bystanders with the capacity to recognize and respond to witnessed bias, as well as be aware of potentially enacting bias ourselves. Rather than dictate information in a top-down approach, we wanted to practice more active pedagogy by incorporating a combination of content delivery, small-group discussion, collective information sharing and large-group discussion.

That said, none of us had prior experience leading workshops of this scope, and a major concern was how to put this event together responsibly. Our backgrounds are in medieval history, a notoriously white and cis-male field. As we began to plan the workshop, we soon had to confront the fact that all of our mentors in the field, and therefore the people we felt comfortable asking to participate in our faculty panel discussion without monetary compensation, were white. We felt that it was irresponsible to host a workshop on equity, diversity and bias in academia with an entirely white faculty panel. However, asking scholars of color to contribute uncompensated labor for the benefit of our workshop would also be irresponsible and tokenizing. In this, we were encountering firsthand the results of gatekeeping academic hiring practices that have historically excluded scholars of color from medieval and other pre-modern fields.

In an attempt to counterbalance the racial homogeneity of the faculty panel, we sought to include resources throughout the workshop that centered different identities and perspectives in terms of race, academic position and research focus. We also addressed directly the lack of racial and ethnic diversity in the workshop at the beginning of the day's programming. In keeping with the collaborative environment of the day, we asked participants to reflect on what we could have done differently, and how they might approach this situation if they ever find themselves in a similar one. For those of us in academia with racial privilege, it is imperative to seek out solutions that invite and include diverse perspectives into the conversation.

2   The Workshop

Our workshop ran for one full day, and the audience included primarily pre-modern studies undergraduate students and faculty members. Because the workshop was open to all undergraduates, however, we worked to design sessions that would be widely applicable outside the study of the pre-modern world, be it in other graduate fields or other workplaces. In taking this conceptual approach, we designed the workshop in such a way that the key takeaways could be learned and then abstracted into lessons relevant to nearly any circumstance of implicit or explicit bias. Below is a discussion of the two main sessions that we hosted, followed by a description of the faculty panel that followed these sessions. In the appendices, we supply a full program schedule as well as activities and discussion questions referred to below and used throughout the workshop. Our hope is that such appendices will further illuminate the nuts and bolts of the day's programming, and may serve as a tool or reference for any other graduate students planning a similar workshop.

We opened our workshop with a session called "Navigating Bias in the Academy." This first session specifically focused on recognizing bias and abuse of power structures within academia. Since we all grow up with biases ingrained in us by our communities, families and cultures, it may seem like a simple task to identify such biases. Nonetheless, it is often difficult to recognize bias when it manifests as "small" incidents that we are accustomed to dismissing or normalizing. These incidents, however, play a large role in systemic discrimination, elevating traditional white male voices and mentalities while keeping people with marginalized backgrounds and perspectives from rising to positions of power and equality, particularly as graduate students, postdoctoral researchers and professors.

For example, as a graduate student, an individual has different roles and responsibilities daily. They might be a student, a teacher and a researcher; or an intern and a student; or a student who is also a full-time working professional. As they move throughout their day, a graduate student likely transitions among these different roles, beginning their day as a teacher, for instance, and ending it as a student attending class. One of the challenges of balancing these various roles is the unique position of power and authority that each entails. As they move between these spaces, a graduate student will take on different positions of power in their relationships with others, thereby changing how they experience potential issues of sexual harassment, racial bias, gender bias, etc. Our goal in this session was to discuss these shifting power dynamics with the undergraduates, and to share and brainstorm responses to bias. On a personal level, we each felt underprepared in this respect when we arrived at

graduate school, so we focused on this important skill from the very start of
the workshop.

In this first session on recognizing and responding to bias, we broke into
small groups to brainstorm possible power dynamics and how graduate students with diverse identities fit into such dynamics. After a brainstorming
session in groups, we wrote a list on the board of different kinds of power relationships. Here is a sampling of what we collected:

– Professor/student
– TA/student
– Upper level student/lower level student
– Older student/younger student
– Younger student/older student
– Tenured faculty/untenured faculty
– Supervisor/student
– Extrovert/introvert
– Hierarchy based on perceived prestige of undergraduate school
– Male/female/non-binary
– White/Black, Indigenous, Person of Color (BIPOC)
– Well-known research focus/niche research focus
– Local student/international student
– Neurodivergent/neurotypical
– Disabled/non-disabled

We talked openly about how to react when we find ourselves in abusive or
subtly unhealthy dynamics within these power structures, particularly when
the other person(s) involved do not perceive the bias at hand. Then, we shared
three case studies focused on unhealthy dynamics within academia to dive
deeper into recognizing bias within certain power structures and identifying
possible responses, such as removal from the situation and self-recognition
that the situation was not one's own "fault" (see Appendix 1).

In summary, the exercise was designed to help both students and faculty
members in attendance to recognize shifting vulnerabilities and privilege
within these power structures, and to thereby develop an awareness not only
to recognize when they are a recipient of bias, but also when they may be
unwittingly perpetuating or enacting bias themselves. For those teaching, such
an awareness can be particularly beneficial in moderating classroom partici-
pation in order to create a more equitable environment where diverse voices
and perspectives feel welcome and encouraged.

Moving forward in the day, the second session of the workshop focused on
resource-sharing and discussion for building more equitable academic spaces.

We structured the information of this second half according to the three roles that the graduate might inhabit as discussed in the first half of the day: the student, the teacher and the scholar.

First, our discussion of the "graduate student" focused on formal and informal sources of support in the face of gender-based bias or assault. A campus officer from the Title IX Office—responsible for ensuring university compliance with US federal law that protects individuals from sex-based discrimination—presented information on the emotional and legal support available through the Title IX Office. During this section, we also acknowledged the potential barriers that students may face in accessing these resources. For example, graduate students may feel dissuaded from reporting acts of bias that involve their advisors or fellow graduate students out of fear of potential retaliation. With this in mind, we talked about some of the student-based campus resources that graduate students may be able to rely on while preserving anonymity, such as campus advocates for survivors of sexual assault, or a campus ombuds office. The undergraduates and early career scholars in the room expressed familiarity with these potential barriers and appreciated the open discussion of alternative avenues for support. While it was invigorating to brainstorm alternatives together, it also served as a stark reminder of how many students experience gender-based bias or assault before even completing their undergraduate degree, let alone embarking on further graduate study.

During the section on the "graduate teacher," we emphasized ways of leading academic spaces that actively try not to marginalize students or fellow participants in the space. Since teaching is typically a requirement for graduate students in American PhD programs, we thought it important to give time for workshop participants to think about and work through the dynamics of leading a classroom. We turned to critical pedagogical resources available through Vanderbilt University's Center for Teaching. We spent some time exploring Vanderbilt's many pedagogical guides, such as "Teaching Race," "Teaching beyond the Gender Binary in the University Classroom" and "Increasing Inclusivity in the Classroom" (Thurber, Harbin & Bandy, 2019; Harbin, 2016; Greer, 2014). Along with the undergraduates, we then collectively sought out resources for specifically forming more critical syllabi, paying attention to what and whom to include in the course content. Here, we turned to the websites of the Medievalists of Color and the Teaching Association for Medieval Studies (TEAMS) for their knowledge and inspiration (Hsy & Orlemanski, 2018; Robinson, 2018). In this part of the workshop, it was great to see how both undergraduates and more senior faculty members re-approached the classroom with new critical pedagogical ideas. As early and former graduate students with varying teaching experiences, it was powerful for us to witness how creating spaces for collective learning and discussion could benefit both students and advanced professors. While it is difficult to gauge any ripple effect from this specific workshop, for us it highlighted the importance of creating these spaces and opportunities as part of the work toward more equitable classrooms—a key component of a more equitable academic workplace.

In our final session on the "graduate scholar," we shared and discussed resources for carrying out research in supposedly "niche" areas within pre-modern academia. These "niche" areas, such as disability, gender and race, can often be treated as peripheral to "real" pre-modern scholarship, making it harder for a scholar's work to be taken seriously; in other words, academia can marginalize scholarship as well as scholars. For students contemplating further graduate study, we wanted to illustrate that finding the sources to pursue traditionally undervalued areas of scholarship is possible, and that communities within academia have, in many cases, already put in the labor of assembling online bibliographies or indices as starting points. We presented two such resources as examples: the Feminae Index, and the History of Disease, Disability and Medicine in Medieval Europe source database. We also shared tools from online community spaces and blogs (such as Sarah Ahmed's Feminist Killjoys blog), as well as funding opportunities that specifically serve financially disadvantaged graduate scholars (such as those offered through Sportula).[3] Based on participant engagement, it appeared that these resources were welcome news to many in the room, and we hope that they have been able to assist those undergraduates who have gone on to further graduate study.

Finally, we drew together our discussion of the graduate student, teacher and scholar with a close-reading of a *Medium* article written by Eugenia Zuroski (2018), associate professor of English at McMaster University: "Holding Patterns: On Academic Knowledge and Labor." While not specifically aimed at pre-modern disciplines, Zuroski's work dissects oppressive dynamics within academia and highlights the conditions necessary for building a more equitable academic space for students and scholars. We asked workshop participants to read this article individually and discuss it in small groups before moving into larger group discussions and engaging with reading questions designed to help unpack Zuroski's work in light of the themes of the workshop (see Appendix 3). Here, we asked participants to engage with the written work of a scholar who has already devoted energy and time to the subject of equity and abuse in academia. Looking back, it would have been beneficial to have had more time to discuss Zuroski's article, as it clearly resonated with many of the participants in the room, some of whom expressed excitement at reading a compelling summation of the very dynamics that they hitherto had trouble finding the words to describe.

To close the day-long workshop, we convened a faculty panel session of five of our mentors and colleagues and asked them to reflect on their positionality and experiences within academia (see Appendix 4). We asked them questions such as: When doing research or teaching, how do you think about your identity in relation to the subjects you research and the students you teach and mentor? How does an awareness of your positionality affect your work? How do you think about minority representation in your work, be it in articles, presentations or in the classroom? Through this conversation, we found that many of our mentors were familiar early on with the position we found ourselves in while planning and putting on this workshop: a sense of being unprepared and possibly unqualified, yet hopeful that our work would lead to change within academia.

One key take-away from the panel session was the pressure to maintain continuous passion for the discipline—in other words, the supposed distinction, lauded in academia, that jobs are not so much jobs, as they are labors of love. While enthusiasm for one's job is not inherently problematic, it becomes burdensome when this expectation of unwavering passion excuses hardships and inequities that graduate students may be facing. This expectation of unfaltering passion is also troubling when it causes feelings of inadequacy or inability—imposter syndrome—in graduate students who aren't as passionate as they "should" be. To combat this expectation, the five panelists recommended drawing clear boundaries between one's work and one's passions.

Another highlight from the discussion was a shared concern and frustration among the panelists that far too often the extra, "para-academic" work falls to persons (especially women) of color. While such work is necessary for the health of the academic workplace, this extra labor consequently keeps those individuals from the research and writing that moves their careers forward. For prospective graduate students, the panelists recommended that the students enter academia with a clear awareness of their personal willingness and capacity to perform extra labor.

This panel discussion was a great conclusion to the workshop because it further broke down barriers between faculty and students, both undergraduate and graduate, and gave the undergraduate students a window onto the upsides and downsides of an academic career. All too often, this kind of institutional knowledge goes unspoken, and the ropes must be relearned again and again as new faces enter the field. For students from minority backgrounds, the starting line at the beginning of the search for institutional knowledge may be even further back. The panelists were exceedingly open in sharing their own experiences, and we hope that the tips and tricks they shared to survive and thrive in academia can be passed on to incoming students, especially those of diverse identities.

3   Concluding Reflections

Reflecting on our experience of planning and leading this workshop, we are proud of the result that we achieved. We did our best to organize an event that reflected diversity without tokenizing; that provided resources without embracing solely a content-delivery format; and served as a meaningful experience that somehow moved beyond the ephemeral one-day workshop. The students and faculty who attended were committed to centering diverse thought and minimizing bias in the pre-modern academic field. The students who participated left with the skills to recognize and respond to different forms of bias, preparing them to enter graduate school better able to advocate for themselves and support their peers. Our panelist mentors (one of whom returned from research leave specifically for our workshop) generously engaged with our questions and were willing to share their personal experiences with the group. Above all, we were honored to go back to our alma mater to engage with both undergraduates and faculty and carve out a space for discussing diversity and inclusion in pre-modern disciplines.

This isn't to say, however, that we don't still wonder what constitutes the lasting impact of the workshop, or indeed perhaps of all one-day diversity training workshops. The audience was a self-selected group of students who wanted to spend a day (on a Saturday, no less) learning how to confront bias in academia. Nobody in the room was unaware of the issues of diversity and inclusion in academic spaces. After four months of work, countless hours of team planning, individual preparation, and plane rides across the state, it was hard not to wonder whether we invested too much labor for something relatively "small," because meaningful, actualized diversity and inclusion work should not be assigned to just one day. Instead, this work should be modeled and discussed by the visible, secure figures of the department or university who commit to this work on a regular basis. This needs to be done in classrooms, during office hours and in administrative meetings, where identifying bias and creating more equitable contexts have the greatest possibility for effecting change.

In conclusion, we realize that possible participant responses, or key take-aways from the different program modules, might be missing. Thinking back on the workshop, we remember with certainty that many participants—undergraduates and faculty alike—offered critical, illuminating and self-reflective comments on these difficult topics of bias and abuse in academia. But what we, as the three current and former graduate students who organized, planned and led this event, remember, is the immense labor we invested, the stress and worry during the actual workshop, and the overwhelming relief when the day had successfully concluded. We realize now that we could not meaningfully join in the communal discussions because we were so focused on simply carrying out the logistics of the event. This is part of the reason why we include the four appendices that follow, to fill in the gaps where our collective memory is lacking.

Finally, if we're truly honest in our reflections, our hopes for the realization of a more diverse and equitable academic world are slight and waning. It is possible, however, that such a negative outlook is in part a response to our current times in the US (early 2020), which are characterized by the coronavirus pandemic, institutional anti-Black racism and a tyrannical president. The current exceptional circumstances notwithstanding, it is disheartening to constantly witness the lack of diversity that predominates in academic spaces, and to observe that incidents of abuse continue to unfold (Cassens Weiss, 2020; Loupeda, 2020). Yet, ever hopeful, we hold on to the aspiration of an academic world free of bias and abuse. To arrive here will require that diversity training be seen not as peripheral, but rather as integral to the classroom, the university and the discipline(s). This means assigning credit (or other inducements) for diversity learning, and incorporating diversity and inclusivity work into everyday practices. This also requires that all levels of the academic world nurture greater humility: the humility to listen to the unique perspectives of diverse students and scholars; to self-interrogate; and to welcome changes in behavior that was never really okay, but rather more widely ignored and accepted in the academic spaces of previous times. Perhaps then we will make concrete steps toward ensuring a more just academia.

Publisher's Note

The identity of one of the authors of this chapter has been anonymized. Brill is aware of the real identity of the author. The inclusion of anonymized chapters has been permitted by Brill in view of risks to the general security of the author.

Notes

1   See, for instance, Perlata (2019), and the remarks in solidarity with Perlata by Chaganti (2019),
    providing links to many other relevant pieces.
2   We would like to thank two other women who invested their aid, labor and resources in
    helping us organize this workshop.
3   *Feminae: Medieval Women and Gender Index.* Society for Medieval Feminist Scholarship.
    https://inpress.lib.uiowa.edu/feminae/WhatIsFeminae.aspx; *History of Disease, Disability,
    and Medicine in Medieval Europe,* https://dishist.hypotheses.org/; *The Sportula: Microgrants
    for Classics Students,* https://thesportula.wordpress.com/. See also Ahmed (2017).

References

Ahmed, S. (2017, December 19). Diversity work as complaint. *Feministkilljoys.*
    https://feministkilljoys.com/2017/12/19/diversity-work-as-complaint/
Cassens Weiss, D. (2020, June 2). Stanford law prof who used quote with racial slur
    in class says he won't do it again. *AbaJournal.* https://www.abajournal.com/news/
    article/stanford-law-prof-who-used-quote-with-racial-slur-in-class-says-he-wont-
    do-it-again
Chaganti, S. (2019, January 18). On context: AIA-SCS 2019. *Medievalists of Color.*
    https://medievalistsofcolor.com/public-discourse/
Greer, A. (2014). Increasing inclusivity in the classroom. *Vanderbilt University Center
    for Teaching.* https://cft.vanderbilt.edu/guides-sub-pages/increasing-inclusivity-
    in-the-classroom/
Harbin, B. (2016). *Teaching beyond the gender binary in the university classroom.*
    Updated by L. M. Roberts et al. (2020). Vanderbilt Center for Teaching.
    https://cft.vanderbilt.edu/guides-sub-pages/teaching-beyond-the-gender-
    binary-in-the-university-classroom/#cred
Hsy, J., & Orlemanski, J. (2018). Race and medieval studies: A partial bibliography.
    Medievalists of Color. https://medievalistsofcolor.com/resources/pedagogy-
    bibliographies/
Loupeda, M. (2020, May 11). Students call for accountability, faculty diversity after pro-
    fessor twice uses racial slur. *Stanford Daily.*
    https://www.stanforddaily.com/2020/05/11/students-call-for-accountability-
    faculty-diversity-after-professor-twice-uses-racial-slur/
Perlata, D. P. (2019, January 7). Some thoughts on AIA-SCS 2019. *Medium.* https://
    medium.com/@danelpadillaperalta/some-thoughts-on-aia-scs-2019-d6a480a1812a
Robinson, C. L. (2018). *Featured lesson resource page: Race, racism, and the Middle Ages.*
    Teaching Association for Medieval Studies (TEAMS). https://teams-medieval.org/
    ?page_id=76

Thurber, A., Harbin, M. B., & Bandy, J. (2019). Teaching race: Pedagogy and practice. *Vanderbilt University Center for Teaching.* https://cft.vanderbilt.edu/teaching-race/

Zuroski, E. (2018, April 5). Holding patterns: On academic knowledge and labor. *Medium.* https://medium.com/@zugenia/holding-patterns-on-academic-knowledge-and-labor-3e5a6oooecbf

Appendix 1: Schedule (Created by Hanna McGinnis, Ana C. Núñez and Anonymous 4)

Breakfast (9:30–10:00)

Session I (10:00 AM–12:00 PM): Navigating Bias in the Academy
The intention of this half of the program is to begin talking in more general terms about gender and other bias and power dynamics in academia; to outline potential formal and informal resources that students and scholars can draw from when deciding how to respond to bias; to discuss strategies for how to support colleagues experiencing bias; and to discuss strategies for ensuring against (unintentionally) marginalizing one's colleagues. This more general half of the program will be complemented by the second half (see Session II below), in which we will seek specific answers from an academic panel.

1. (10 minutes) Introduction: Intentions and Goals
2. (40 minutes) Power Dynamics in the Academy and Recognizing Bias:
    - i. Activity I: Small groups to brainstorm dynamics encountered in an academic setting. Here we will encourage the students to think critically about more nuanced situations.
    - ii. Activity II: Coming together as a room to share thoughts. The master list compiled will serve as a reminder throughout the event that will be crucial in the second half of the program. The session leaders will then discuss how bias plays into the broader hierarchical dynamics of academia.
    - iii. The session leaders will speak to personal experiences of bias and the support or resistance they encountered when deciding whether to confront it.
3. (10 minutes) Morning Break
4. (60 minutes) Toolkit for Responding to Bias:
    - i. Speaker I: A speaker from the university's center for prevention, advocacy and support for survivors of sexual violence and harassment will discuss relevant campus resources.
    - ii. Speakers II: The session leaders will discuss additional resources, highlighting communities (both in person and online), gathering support systems and allies, and the power of collective action.

iii.   Activity III: Bias Bibliography. Session leaders will present a few blogs, book chapters and (online) groups as potentially helpful resources for students and scholars.

iv.   Activity IV: Small groups (2–3 people), brainstorming strategies for supporting colleagues experiencing bias, highlighting how to proactively offer support and how to respond when someone reaches out for support.

v.   Activity V: Coming together as a room to share thoughts culminating in the composition of a second master list.

vi.   Activity VI: Small groups (2–3 people), brainstorming how students and scholars can attempt to proactively and meaningfully prevent the further marginalization of students and scholars in these fields.

vii.   Activity VII: Coming together as a room to share thoughts and build another master list.

LUNCH (12:00 PM–1:00 PM) Over lunch everyone will be asked to write down one or two questions for the culminating discussion.

Session II (1:00 PM–4:00 PM): Research and Teaching

The intention of this half of the program is to look at identity and bias in academia through the lens of research and teaching. The academic panel will give scholars and researchers the opportunity to share their experiences in academia, their approach to pursuing research and teaching, and their assessments of how their fields can be expanded. This session will culminate in an interactive discussion in which everyone in the room will have a chance to ask questions or propose answers.

1.   (100 minutes) Panel on Research and Teaching
    a.   Panel speakers will each be provided with a list of questions beforehand from which they can choose several or all to address.
2.   (15 minutes) Afternoon Break
3.   (45 minutes) This concluding session will give the students and the panelists the opportunity to engage in a fully interactive manner with the material covered throughout the day. The questions that the students brainstorm over lunch will be used to fuel this discussion in the case that lulls arise between questions/comments.
4.   (20 minutes) Conclusion/Final share-out.

Appendix 2: Case Studies (Created by Hanna McGinnis, Ana C. Núñez and Anonymous 4)

1.   Your advisor asks you how you're habituating to the new environment of grad school. You share your fears of being less prepared than your classmates, at

which point your advisor tells you to be more confident and to "man-up" and act the part of a graduate student, since this is no longer an undergraduate environment that will baby you as you go.

a. How does this comment make you feel? Would you leave the meeting feeling better/more prepared than you entered?

b. Is this an example of a productive advisor/student meeting? Why or why not?

c. How might you continue this meeting?

d. Would knowing the gender identity of the people involved in this scenario change how you view the situation?

2. One day before class starts, you overhear Student A brag to Student B about how much Student A has already written for an upcoming paper assignment. Student A then asks Student B how much they have written. Student B responds, nervously, saying that they have finished their research and have an outline, but still need to write the paper. Student A laughs dismissively, saying Student B must be struggling to keep up with the workload, which wasn't designed to accommodate everyone's abilities.

a. Would you engage in this conversation, and if so, how and with what intention?

b. If not, what might you say to Student B after the conversation with Student A has ended?

c. Do you consider this conversation to be unhealthy? Why or why not?

3. At the 2017 International Medieval Congress at Leeds, when introducing the keynote lecture on the theme of "otherness," which was part of a panel of white, European men speaking on the topic, the moderator joked that "If audience members thought he was just another old, white man, they should just wait until after his holiday at the beach." https://www.chronicle.com/article/ Medievalists-Recoiling-From/240666

a. How does this comment make you feel?

b. Imagine that after the conference, people are discussing the event, and a colleague says that they don't see anything wrong with the comment and think people were overreacting since it was "just a joke." Do you feel able to further discuss this situation with your colleague? If so, what might you say?

c. What might be an appropriate way to introduce an all-white and male panel on otherness?

Appendix 3: Reading Questions (Created by Hanna McGinnis, Ana C. Núñez and Anonymous 4)

Eugenia Zuroski, "Holding Patterns: On Academic Knowledge and Labor," Medium.com, Apr 5 2018, https://medium.com/@zugenia/holding-patterns-on-academic-knowledge-and-labor-3e5a6oooecbf

Reading Questions

1. "If we want to build solidarity within hostile institutional conditions, we must do better at respecting all knowledge formed at particular distances from power, especially when it addresses us directly."

    a.   What might respecting this knowledge look like?

2. "[S]ome of us are compeled structurally to perform kinds of labor that others of us have never come to know, or not until now."

    a.   What might this (often unacknowledged) labor look like?
    b.   In what ways do you think students/scholars with more privilege could ease the burden placed on students/scholars with less privilege to perform this kind of labor?

3. "[S]ometimes I have been part of this 'we,' and sometimes I have been the 'you.' I have tried to learn by listening."

    a.   Imagining yourself to be part of this "we," what might be ways of resisting "hostile institutional conditions" (quoted from first excerpt)?
    b.   Imagining yourself to be part of this "you," can you think of gaps in your knowledge/experience, and ways you could educate yourself or be more open to listening? What do you think is at stake in listening to folks whose experience differs from your own?

4. "Academic allyship has to be focused on transforming institutions, overhauling their missions and methods, to make them worthy of the people they mobilize and claim to serve. We don't need your admiration, your acclaim, your invitation. We don't need you to feel bad. We need you to hire more of us; we need you to practice humility; we need you to take some instruction. There's a collective

endeavor underway, and we're showing you this: step away from the center and you'll learn how to do the work."

a.   What might "step[ping] away from the center" look like?
b.   Where do you think undergraduate and graduate students fit into academic allyship and transforming institutions?
c.   Where do you think graduate students who don't intend to go further in academia fit into academic allyship and transforming institutions?

Appendix 4: Faculty Panel Questions (Created by Hanna McGinnis, Ana C. Núñez and Anonymous 4)

1.   *Personal Introduction*: Please introduce yourself to the group. When and why did you realize you wanted to pursue graduate studies and a career in academia? What was that experience like? How did you first encounter your research interests?

2.   *Positionality*: When doing research or teaching, how do you think about your identity in relation to the subjects you research and the students you teach and mentor? How does an awareness of your positionality affect your work? How do you think about minority representation in your work, be it in articles, presentations or in the classroom?

3.   *"Standard" versus "peripheral" history*: Within pre-modern studies, are there certain types of history that might be seen as "standard" (e.g., military, economic, political), and others that might be seen as "peripheral" (e.g., gender, sexuality, environmental)? What are the trends regarding these "two camps," if such a divide exists? Do ideas of "standard" versus "peripheral" history also emerge based on the kind of platform used (e.g., Speculum versus Eidolon)? Or based on the identity of the historian (e.g., white male versus brown woman)?

4.   *Advice to potential graduate students*: Thinking back on your experience as a graduate student and now a professor, and bearing in mind the theme of today's workshop—navigating gender and other identities in the Academy—what advice would you give to students thinking about pursuing graduate studies in the humanities? What lessons or words of encouragement would you like to leave them with today?

CHAPTER 11

Still a World to Win

Anonymous 5

When I entered the Dutch academic world as a young (male) scholar in 1983, I expected to become part of a broad-minded, open community in which thoughts and ideas would be exchanged. Nothing could have been further from the truth. I became part of a world in which scholarly ideas were hardly ever exchanged and open discussions barely possible. Moreover, there were many conflicts between my colleagues, on a professional as well as personal level. Many of these were over power and status, and they often arose from jealousy and frustration over the success of other scholars and/or those in positions of authority within the university. Within this strange world, I have always done my best to go my own way, to stay true to myself and to treat my colleagues and students with the respect they deserve, regardless of gender, background and skin color. Hopefully I have succeeded in this.

At the time of my entry into academia, it was much more hierarchical than it is now. Full professors (most of them male) were at the top of the hierarchy and wielded considerable power over everyone lower in the pecking order. Fortunately, that has changed somewhat over the years, and now the voices of those lower in the hierarchy are also being heard. Yet full professors still exercise substantial authority and sometimes abuse their power. I am sorry to say that, in my experience at least, the increased number of female full professors over the past decades does not appear to have improved this situation. Like men, women in positions of authority sometimes behave in intimidating ways towards those below them in the hierarchy.

Fortunately, I have seldom been a victim of abuse of power and intimidation in my academic career. I remember only one such occasion, which had a great impact on me personally. The incident occurred in the early 1990s, as I was gradually becoming successful as a scholar and administrator within my department and the faculty of arts. My boss at the time had, as a young scholar, seemed to have a promising career ahead but did not live up to expectations. In the beginning, he supported me unreservedly, but our relationship gradually deteriorated with my growing success. We had disagreements and he tried to thwart my career. Our differences of opinion increased and I was regularly the target of his fits of anger. I thus avoided him as much as possible. The shit really hit the fan one day when he stormed into my office because I had apparently

© JULIE HANSEN AND INGELA NILSSON, 2022 | DOI:10.1163/9789004521025_011

said or done something that was not to his liking. He started bullying me and said, "I am the professor here. I make the decisions, and you do as I tell you." I was shocked and asked him to leave my office. I filed a formal complaint about his inappropriate behavior, shown towards others as well as towards me. I think he received a formal reprimand. After that, we avoided one another and were no longer on speaking terms. These strained relations gave me cause to seriously consider leaving academia, but I'm glad I didn't. Fortunately, over the last decades academia has become more open, broad-minded, diverse and less hierarchical, even though there is still a world to win.

Publisher's Note

The author's identity is anonymized for this chapter. Brill is aware of the real identity of the author. The inclusion of anonymized chapters has been permitted by Brill in view of risks to the general security of the author.

CHAPTER 12

Fragments of Missed Opportunities

Or Unrealized Dialectical Exchanges with a Mentor

Anonymous 6

1   What Was Said

18/06/20xx, 23:50: Dear Denis,[1] I will be in my office tomorrow morning. Come see me, I need to talk to you. Professor
19/06/20xx, 00:02: Dear Professor, Of course. I hope it is nothing serious. See you tomorrow. Denis

P: ... remember, last summer, in the restaurant by the sea, when most of the others had left, you were washing your hands in the bathroom and I approached you from behind. You leaned towards me, but suddenly pulled back when you heard a noise ... [leans forward expectantly]
D: I'm really sorry, professor. I remember that dinner, but I really cannot recall the moment you refer to. I'm sorry if I ... [the rest of the record has been censored by survival mechanisms]

19/06/20xx, 20:45: Dear Professor, I am a bit troubled by what you mentioned this morning. But only because I'm afraid you might be troubled, too. I was trying really hard to remember what I did, and it is true that I recall a moment of proximity that might have caused the confusion. And it is my fault. On the one hand, you must have noticed that I am rather flirtatious in general and, on the other, I am used to combining intellectual closeness with certain physical gestures. Anyhow, I am glad you mentioned it, since honesty and sincerity are qualities I really appreciate in you. Please know that, from the very start, you have been a great father figure to me, and you remain someone I respect, admire and—moreover—am inspired by. As a student, friend and confidant, I remain at your disposal.
Cordially, D.

19/06/20xx, 20:45: Dear Denis, no troubles, no problems, no worries. A long road lies ahead of us. We talk, we explain, we live. A very important thing: I

© JULIE HANSEN AND INGELA NILSSON, 2022 | DOI:10.1163/9789004521025_012

found a copy of my book, come pick it up on Monday. Complicitly yours, and please, no father figures—I despise them. P.

2   What Could Have Been Said

2.1   *Fragment I*

P: What did you want to discuss?

D: Sexuality, rapaciousness and academia.

P: Why now?

D: Because the long road is over and you have no power over my life anymore.

P: You were always a strong and stubborn person. What kind of power have I ever had over you?

D: You arranged for me to relocate to a foreign country whose language I barely spoke, to a city where I had no social support, to enter a system where I always felt slightly illegal, did not know my rights or the administrative mechanisms. You convinced me to pursue a long unfunded endeavor without any structure, but with you as the sole reference point in a foreign land.

P: When I was your age, I traveled Europe alone! Did I tell you about that time in a monastery?

D: Many times. You also told me not to worry about money because you would help me figure something out. I don't know whether I prefer to believe that you were just lying, or that you had some kind of sleazy arrangement in mind.

P: You were always so sensitive and creative. I don't know where you get your ideas. You were always neurotic about money, too. You seemed to be doing just fine.

D: I was lucky to meet genuinely generous people. I was also motivated enough to juggle three jobs at a time. You call me neurotic, but while you got a bonus for having an extra student, I had to get by at times with half the minimum wage.

P: You're exaggerating, reducing a fruitful scholarly relation to a moment of physical weakness. My students are everything to me.

D: Scaffoldings for your robust ego?

P: Would not life have been harder for you in your country, where you could not express yourself freely?

D: You made sure to establish that early on, didn't you?

P: Whatever do you mean?

D: You asked my colleague if I was homosexual less than a week after you met me.

2.2   *Fragment II*

P: I felt you needed support, encouragement and acceptance. I felt I could empathize with your position.

D: I was in my early twenties and living my sexuality more or less openly. You were nearly retired, married, with children, inquiring about other people's sexuality by proxy.

P: You are twisting words and events. I was genuinely caring.

D: I believed you were caring, now I know you were tentacular.

P: I accepted you and appreciated you as you were.

D: You imagined me as you wanted me to be. You were being duplicitous. You said you had two sons and that, if you had a third one, you would like him to be just like me. And I told that to all my friends as a wonderful example of kindness and acceptance in academia. That is, before you made your move and tried to convince me that I misconstrued you as a father figure, or whatever.

2.3   *Fragment III*

P: I do not see anything wrong in a physical relationship between two free and equal adults.

D: Then why did you wait for your wife to leave the city before approaching me?

P: There's no need to bring her into this, this is between a teacher and a student.

D: I'm sorry to ruin your Spartan fantasy, but you have just tapped the nerve of inequality in our positions as adults.

P: You are being so Anglo-Saxon and puritan! This bureaucratic temperament will be the death of free academia. Makes me wonder what happened to the spirit of '68!

D: Mind your adjectives! What was this spirit of '68, pray you?

P: Freeing bodies, unbinding spirits, unshackling minds! Society and academia have forgotten our great heritage.

D: And where were you while they were forgetting? Having a perfectly heteronormative life, dipping your spoon into the sexual liberties in the cupboard, cashing in on social democracy, while letting it expire and disintegrate.

P: But the spirit of freedom ...

D: Freedom begins where necessity ends. How was I to live my freedom with homophobes on one side and predators on the other, both latently threatening my physical integrity?

2.4   *Fragment IV*

P: You're accusing me of heterowhatever, while you defend a puritan traditionalism that only allows for relations sanctioned by bourgeois society.

D: It's the dishonest predatory types that keep us trapped in our "chosen" binary categories, because we feel it is safer there. Sexuality is the most liberating thing there is. But you cannot blame me for not wanting to explore the depths of a shark tank.

2.5   *Fragment V*

D: You know the joke you always tell about northern cavemen and southern faggots in antiquity?

P: Brilliant, isn't it?

D: It's about as funny as the one about a woman's head serving as a beer-pint stand.

2.6   *Fragment VI*

P: You're turning this into a trial.

D: I could have, had I wanted to.

P: So, I should just stop doing young people favors to avoid hurting their feelings?

D: You know, I hooked up with a guy soon after I met you, just before starting my studies. An "uneducated" fellow, professional waiter. Dazzled by the opportunity you offered, I bragged so much about being lucky, about the things you said and your warm endorsement. "Just you wait," he said, "soon he will name his price." No way, I objected, not in academia!

P: What is the meaning of this?

D: The meaning is that you are not extraordinary in any way, and that the ivory tower is porous and rotten.

P: Do you think you are special?

D: No, now I know that I was not the first one to refuse you.

2.7   *Fragment VII*

P: You just want to hurt me.

D: I just wish I could unhurt myself.

2.8   *Fragment VIII*

P: Why are you so obsessed with this? It happened years ago and I didn't even touch you!

D: You touched me and others inappropriately so many times. And you always stood too close.

P: You did not object.

D: Was I in a position to object?

P: Now you are being duplicitous. On top of perverting an honest affection, if this vision of frigid and sterile academia is what you believe in, why didn't you fight for it?

D: Even if we disregard the fact that I felt my career and livelihood were at stake, there are still a couple of reasons.

P: I would never cause you harm.

D: You were doing it constantly without realizing it.

P: What are the other reasons?

D: Insecurity and empathy.

2.9   *Fragment IX*

P: Do you think it was easy for me? Do you know where and when I grew up? It's easy for you to talk about freedom.

D: Do not turn this into a generational thing. Do you remember that famous scholar from our field who admitted his attraction to a male colleague? His boss "found him a wife" to quiet down the rumors, because the object of his attraction bullied and blackmailed him, threatening to ruin a joint project. Do you know that less renowned scholar from our field who fled the dictatorship and jubilantly lived his homosexuality for decades, with or without his partner, without harassing or harming anyone around him? They are both of your generation, living in the same city. Alternatives become more obvious when you move the axis of the world away from yourself.

2.10   *Fragment X*

P: Now you are being duplicitous. You admitted to being flirtatious.

D: And you did nothing to correct me.

2.11   *Fragment XI*

P: You always had a nasty character. And this dialogue is artless, you turned me into a scarecrow, a one-dimensional caricature that no one can empathize with. I don't understand what kind of empathy you are talking about.

D: That afternoon, after you stood too close to me once again, while I was thinking of ways to mend my vulnerability, when I did not know whom to ask for advice, when I dug painfully deep into my memories and forced myself to fill the void with your version of events, a part of me that was not torn between panic and anger and guilt, a part of me was actually feeling compassion for you.

P: You were pitying me?

D: I was trying to put myself in your thick skin. I imagined myself 30 years on, an emotionally hungry male professor in frigid academia, tortured by the fact that he happened to be attracted to male beauty and youth in front of him, nostalgic for the beauty and youth that he wasted laboring behind dusty volumes.

P: Your brain is too complicated. Didn't you get anything from me?

D: Oh, so much! A life-long warning and empathy for those who deserve it. When I opened up to my friends, I heard so many stories of unsolicited exposures, implicit blackmail, wandering hands, rapes. Years later, I told my mother about what you did. She shared stories of sexual harassment by her professors. I was the first person she ever dared talk to about this.

2.12   *Fragment XII*

P: You admitted to being flirtatious. You're a bright young man, you knew what you were doing.

D: Throughout my education I overheard and imagined whispers. They said I was gay because I wore a different outfit every day. They said I was sucking up to professors because I always asked questions. They said my grades were higher than what I actually deserved. They said I got where I was through charm and rhetoric, they said I had no substance. And here I was, starting out in a new environment, being told that the man who brought me there was interested in my body. Were you ever aware that I disagreed with most of your scholarly work? Did you even hear anything of what I said?

P: You are twisting and projecting. You make it sound like I violated you.

D: Should I be grateful that you didn't?

2.13   *Fragment XIII*

P: Your brain is too complicated. My students are all over the world, I gave all I had to them. Didn't you get anything from me?

D: You turned me into a monster from my father's nightmares. I spent my whole adult life secretly trying to prove to him that queer relations are not necessarily "tainted" with perversion, illicit seduction and exploitation of youth, falling into the decency trap. I thought I carved a stable ground for myself, a safe social niche. And at the beginning of my independent life, there I was, losing at my own game.

P: I couldn't have known any of these things.

D: Would you have done anything differently if you had?

Note

1   The name is fictitious.

CHAPTER 13

Flexing Muscles

Ingela Nilsson

> A smile is formed primarily by flexing the muscles at the sides of the mouth. [...] Among humans, a smile expresses pleasure, sociability, happiness, joy or amusement. It is distinct from a similar but usually involuntary expression of anxiety known as a grimace.
>
> "SMILE" (Wikipedia, n.d.)

∵

Looking back over some thirty years in academia, I sometimes wonder if there has been more focus on my facial expressions than on my research. It all started, I think, with a piece of friendly advice. I was on the shortlist for a position and was to be interviewed by a panel. The day before the interview one of my close colleagues and friends offered me some advice. She told me to relax and be confident, then added, "And don't look so sour, it will be off-putting to the panel, you have to start looking more friendly, smile a bit!" I remember my instantaneous annoyance: who was she to imply I always look sour? And anyway, even if it were true, I had good reason to look sour, after years of pointless criticism from colleagues who found faults with whatever I did. And even if I looked sour for no good reason, it was my face, I had the right to look however I wanted! But she insisted, to the point that I understood that this was a common conception of me: I was an angry and sour-looking person, who risked my career unless I took control of my facial muscles and started to smile.

Since I was an angry and sour-looking person who insisted that I had the right to be that way, I did not smile at the interview. I was offered the position nevertheless, but my well-intentioned colleague's comment echoed at the back of my mind and I began taking mental note of similar advice from other colleagues. I also started recalling such occasions in the past. The co-student who told me to stop looking so angry, since it would scare away people—especially men. The professor who called me aggressive when I questioned his critique, claiming he was afraid to spend time alone with me. The supervisor who told me to cheer up and smile more, assuring me it would make people be nicer in

© INGELA NILSSON, 2022 | DOI:10.1163/9789004521025_013

return. The colleague who told me that I acted like a grumpy teenager, because I didn't sufficiently admire the environment of the posh research institute and never smiled at the director. The mentor of the pedagogical course who suggested that a smile would make my teaching more enjoyable. Had I always been an angry and sour-looking person who put people off with my facial expression? If so, why did my friends and quite a few colleagues accept me the way I was without questioning my personality? I was perfectly happy, so why did people keep telling me to cheer up?

I began spending time in front of the mirror, flexing and unflexing my facial muscles. It was quite true, I realized, that when my face was completely relaxed I looked rather sour, sort of like when I was fourteen. I practiced ways of flexing the muscles at the sides of my mouth so that I looked friendlier, without quite smiling. I wanted to look friendly, though I refused to humor my critics by smiling. After months (or was it years?) of practicing, I noticed a certain difference in my surroundings: I was clearly seen as less intimidating, even if I did not actually smile much. It was an astonishing discovery. What basic insight of the human mind had escaped me, and only me, for so many years?

The careful study of my own face made me much more aware of other people's expressions and it slowly dawned on me that most people never relaxed
their facial muscles. They must have learned something earlier in life that I
had missed. Women in particular had splendid control over their faces. Their
eyes were constantly wide open and the corners of their mouths turned lightly
upwards, lending a friendly curiosity to their appearance. To me it seemed
rather exhausting, especially the eye thing. And several women also seemed
to smile while talking, an exercise that appeared not only exhausting but also
to affect their voices. Some of them looked as if they were caught in an eter-
nal grimace, which was more frightening than friendly to me. Men clearly had
other ways to flex their muscles, physically and intellectually, so they didn't
care as much about their faces. On the other hand it seemed as if their facial
expressions were of less concern to others, and they were certainly interpreted
differently. A wrinkled forehead was not a sign of an aggrieved personality, but
gave character to a male face. A raised eyebrow signaled ironic distance, not
sarcastic critique. And even if quite a few men I observed seemed much more
intimidating than I thought I was, I never heard a man being offered the same
advice that I was: Smile and look friendly, otherwise it will harm your career?
Nah, not really.

I did not become the kind of smiling person that my colleague had perhaps
hoped for; if anything, my observations made me more determined not to give
in, to argue my right to be an unsmiling woman in academia. However, my new
awareness made me so much aware of my "problems" that I learned to put on a
well-practiced friendly face in professional situations simply in order to avoid
accusations of being unfriendly. After a decade or so I no longer thought much
about it, except for when I accidentally caught a glimpse of my relaxed face in
the reflection of a window and remembered to properly flex the muscles at the
sides of my mouth. I was careful never to let my half-smile turn into a smirk
or a grimace and I really tried to avoid the involuntary tick of raising my right
eyebrow, which apparently (so I was told) made it seem as if I was mocking the
speaker. I wanted to be seen as a friendly person, not an angry woman. There
did not seem to be many other alternatives to choose from. There still aren't.

Although I was very angry at the time, I am now grateful for my colleague's
advice. It was a useful reminder of the way in which women are perceived,
making me very much aware of both gendered power structures and my own
facial muscles. Am I hiding my angry self behind a controlled mask of friend-
liness? I guess I am, allowing her to appear in certain situations that demand
her presence. She is fearful and rather awesome, correct but sarcastic, and she

knows better than anyone that a smile expresses much more than happiness and joy. In fact, she smiles much more than my friendly face does.

Reference

Wikipedia. (n.d.). *Smile*. Retrieved March 29, 2022, from https://en.wikipedia.org/wiki/Smile

CHAPTER 14

Lessons I Learned at University

Ricarda Schier

A while ago I found myself attending an illuminating lecture. A teacher of mine delivered a long monologue about how I, as a young woman, am simply not taken seriously in this world and how I just have to deal with that. He illustrated this with anecdotes of what other men had thought and said about me.

This wasn't exactly news to me. As a woman in academia, I am generally aware, although many won't admit it, that there are still a lot of people who perceive me as less capable because of my gender. Not necessarily because they actually think that women are less intelligent than men, but because a lot of characteristics traditionally framed as female are not associated with rational thinking, while many traits traditionally framed as male are. In other, more personal words: several of the insecurities I had during my time at university stemmed from the fact that when you think of an intellectual, you typically don't think of a young, blonde girl with a high-pitched voice, who laughs a lot and likes to wear short skirts.

For a long time though, I would tell myself it was just that: my own insecurities. Surely I was imagining that patronizing treatment I seemed to receive a lot from mostly older men. Surely I misinterpreted those condescending smiles they gave me when I spoke. However, that all ended the day that teacher mansplained sexism to me. Since receiving that lecture, I am now convinced that I and other women (in academia or elsewhere) are not collectively imagining things, and that if you feel you are not being taken seriously for reasons that have nothing to do with your actual intellectual capacities, you are probably not overreacting—it may simply be the truth. I am perceived as weaker, less smart and less competent because of my gender, at least by some people.

This lecture was, in a painful way, more educational than a lot of the seminars and talks I attended regularly at university. It is a great example of how as a student I learned a lot of uncomfortable lessons about the academic world (and humanity in general). I want to share some of them in case they might be helpful:

Lesson 1. Abuse and harassment come in many different forms and are often not as easy to recognize as one would think, especially not by the victim. Our bodies and minds normally tell us when our boundaries have been violated: we

feel uncomfortable, stressed, threatened, physically nauseous. But our immediate reaction to these feelings is often to question them. We are taught to evaluate things from a rational perspective. Strong emotions, especially negative
ones, are often frowned upon. We don't want to be regarded as hysterical or
weak. When we feel something is very wrong, though, something probably is
wrong. Although it is awkward to talk about an awkward situation, it is really
helpful to talk to other people and get their perspective, because it is often
easier to evaluate a situation that you are not part of yourself. Others can be
quicker to see when we are being treated inappropriately.

Lesson 2. If you want to work in academia, be prepared for exploitation. You
might be exploited by supervisors who steal your work, by fellow students
who steal your work, by other people who steal your work. You might also be
exploited by publishers who profit from the fact that you have to publish in
order to advance in your career but never have to pay you. I'm not saying you
will be exploited, but that you should be prepared.

Lesson 3. Being a brilliant scholar or a good teacher doesn't mean someone is a
great person. It doesn't mean they are kind, or altruistic, or honest. Academia
would be a better place if we paid as much attention to how we treat each
other as how many papers we published; if we valued people for their decency
as much as how big their name is in their field. It is better to stick with the people who are nice and caring, instead of trying at all costs to get close to famous
scholars who you think might advance your career.

Lesson 4. Although you are taught much about objective thinking, constructive
criticism and how to make a professional argument at university, people are
still emotional beings and will take things personally, which is probably why
grown-up scholars sometimes behave like school children. It is a damaging pretense that one must always be rational and free of emotion instead of acknowledging when one feels unnecessarily attacked or provoked. Being more open
and honest with ourselves and others would make working together easier.

Lesson 5. There is no need to be loyal to people or institutions that treat you
badly. We tend to make excuses for people who behave inappropriately. We
don't want to make unfair accusations, we don't want to be regarded as judgmental, or we are simply afraid to make a fuss and are scared that we would
ultimately be the ones who come off looking bad. We may forget, however, that
those people who act abusively or simply unprofessionally are not being forced
to do so. They act in this way because their actions don't have consequences,

and they will continue to act this way until their actions have consequences. This can only happen if someone speaks up.

••

I learned some of these lessons through things that happened to me personally; some I learned through stories I heard from others. Some people told me they are not representative of academia. But then why do I know so many stories from around the world of stolen dissertations, sexual harassment, bullying, sexism, racism, burnout, depression and the ever-present fear of unemployment? There is a lot of gossip and talking behind other people's backs about these kinds of problems; an open conversation about why they occur so frequently at universities is sorely missing. This has much to do with prioritizing work output above everything else—including creating a decent work environment—and valuing only intellectual achievements while ignoring traits like kindness, decency, integrity and professionalism. Moreover, many universities seem to need stronger mechanisms to prevent and deal with abuse. Victims of harassment and bullying are often unsure of where or to whom they can turn for help. Sometimes those they talk to don't believe their situation requires action, or don't believe them at all. Even though it might be hard, having an open conversation about these problems and learning from all of these uncomfortable lessons is the first step toward realizing that the way we treat each other in academia not only can, but must, be better.

CHAPTER 15

Benevolence or Bitterness

Antony T. Smith

I found the pathway to tenure stressful and fraught with tensions, and I know I am not alone in feeling this way. In the American university system, the tenure track races toward a fifth-year tenure file submission and a sixth-year vote by colleagues and administrators on whether to award tenure (i.e. promotion to associate professor) or not to award it (meaning termination of one's assistant professor position). From day one of Fall semester I knew, every moment, that the hourglass was trickling sand slowly and irreversibly until my tenure file submission was due. I am not afraid of hard work, but I soon learned that this high-stakes tenure pathway is not just about effort. Academic expectations, university structures and senior colleagues create tensions deeply rooted in systemic power imbalances. In trying to cope with these tensions while moving toward tenure, the destination became a question about my own emotional and mental state: Would I arrive in a state of benevolence or bitterness?

1   Availability

My PhD advisor tried to give me some advice on my upcoming academic journey as an assistant professor in a tenure-track position. Looking up from a student essay, she peered at me over her reading glasses and stated, "Don't make yourself too available. If you're around campus too much you'll end up doing more service work." I wondered, what would that look like? How would I, as a new hire and assistant professor, make myself scarce while also somehow being regarded as a hardworking and contributing colleague? Should I skip faculty meetings, avoid the program office, or work from home? How many days per week should I work from home? There were no answers to these questions.

I tried to strike a balance between being present and not always being available, but I don't think I was very successful. Course and meeting scheduling interfered with my efforts. As a junior member of the faculty I did not have say in what courses I taught or when I taught them, and as a result my weekly schedule was sometimes a disaster. One semester I had one course that began at 8:30 am and another that started at 4:30 pm, both on the same day, so rather than commuting back and forth from home I stayed on campus—making

© ANTONY T. SMITH, 2022 | DOI:10.1163/9789004521025_015

myself unintentionally available for service work between classes. Faculty meetings were scheduled on Fridays, causing me to lose a prime day for my scholarship and instead be on campus for hours.

Summers were even worse when it came to availability. On nine-month faculty contracts, we do not receive any salary from June through September unless we teach summer term. Described as "optional," teaching summer term was a necessity for me since no matter how much I managed to save I could not go without a paycheck for almost four months. Summer had the university expectation of research, to which it was hard to dedicate much time during the academic year due to teaching and service work—but in summer, this time for research was without compensation. Established senior colleagues used grant funding to support their summer research work, but I had no such grants in my early years. I tried three times to secure an internal grant for this purpose but was denied three years in a row—each proposal taking weeks to write with budget plans I had to develop myself; with each rejection I was left with a denied proposal that added nothing to my curriculum vitae. So I ended up being available to teach courses each summer, needing to pay rent and buy groceries.

In faculty meetings and other interactions I was inevitably asked to join work groups, committees, search committees and task forces. For all my attempts to be less available and to protect time for scholarship, I found I couldn't say no to these requests. Senior colleagues, some of them having been full professors for more than 20 years, were watching, judging my actions to determine my worthiness in academia: Does he work hard? Is he a team player? Is he a valuable colleague? Daring to say no, and making myself less available, had consequences. Saying yes, and taking on service work that would erode my time for scholarship, also had consequences, but only for me, and so this was the path I took, thinking to myself, "I'll find time for my scholarship somewhere. Maybe I can get up earlier, stay up later, or work on weekends." So I said yes to multiple search committees. I said yes to being on a campus-wide writing and communication task force, a group notably populated by junior faculty without institutional knowledge and with the absence of any senior faculty. Clearly these senior colleagues had the agency to say no at times when junior faculty did not, to a series of meetings across an academic year that resulted in a written report promptly ignored by the administration.

The consequences of my inability to say no and to make myself less available extended beyond the workday into what could only be considered personal time. One time a colleague hosted a dinner for a candidate she wanted to impress (and hire). It was scheduled at the last minute and my colleagues and I were expected to come. As it turns out, I had a family commitment I could not cancel, so for once I did say no, and I was the only one who did.

Everyone else attended the dinner, making me look bad. So bad that I ended up taking the candidate to dinner the next night to make up for it, paying for the dinner myself, since the university did not consider the dinner a reimbursable expense. The dinner turned out well, so it seemed that I had managed to salvage this particular situation.

This incident showed me I had to make myself available despite my advisor's words of wisdom, to be at the beck and call of any senior colleague who wanted or needed something, or who wanted me to represent the school at the campus level so that they wouldn't have to and could work on their scholarship instead. One bitter senior colleague, who I ended up referring to as the Viper, invited me to a holiday party at her home. The Viper's unpredictable behavior made me nervous, but I wanted to be on her good side, so I went to the party with my cheerful husband Ken, who I thought might help gloss over any awkwardness at the party. Very few other people were there. While Ken and I stood with our glasses of wine, she came up to us and said, "So good you came! But of course you did, because you want tenure after all, right?" This was followed by a forced and maniacal laugh. I cringed, knowing she was kidding but also that she wasn't. Vipers don't make jokes. She and four other senior colleagues would eventually get to decide my academic future.

2　Imbalance

My inability to make myself less available created an imbalance in my work life. A benevolent senior colleague, whom I nicknamed Grace due to her calm demeanor and ability to speak in complete paragraphs, once acknowledged this work/life imbalance and her own struggles with it. She explained to me, "Tony, this work is, at its very core, mathematically impossible. We are expected to accomplish work in three areas: teaching, scholarship and service. The expectation, really, is 50% teaching, 50% scholarship and 50% service. There's always more work than can possibly be finished." I understood her point, and so for the next five years I did my best to give 150% to my institution, always searching for ways to create more time for scholarship, to work faster, to somehow teach more efficiently despite having to create seven new courses in three years. Being a former school teacher, I couldn't justify cutting corners in teaching—I continued with complex practicum-based assignments for classes of nearly 40 students, without a grader or teaching assistant. I couldn't say no to service work, so I continued to serve on multiple committees and, later, review and editorial boards. I also ended up chairing the curriculum committee, a position of authority ill-suited for junior faculty.

This increasingly severe work/life imbalance took its toll on my scholarship and my personal life. Stacks of unread research journals accumulated in my office and living room; articles and book chapters had to be written at four in the morning, eleven at night, or on weekends when I wasn't grading or planning for class. I missed one grandmother's 90th birthday party, and I seldom visited my other grandmother living in a nursing home. Persistent friends stayed in touch, but the rest faded away, as did all of my hobbies and recreational activities. I didn't have time for them. Ken, a patient man, stayed with me, but years later confessed he got awfully tired of hearing "no" and of going to movies and concerts alone.

At my third-year review, the halfway point to tenure, I was told I wasn't doing enough, feeding a rapidly expanding and overwhelming sense of inadequacy. I needed more publications and, importantly, I needed to get at least one grant—and it had better be a big one. So I stayed up later, got up earlier, worked longer hours on weekends and got a major state-level service grant. This victory made my work imbalance markedly worse, requiring me to travel multiple times over the course of a year to a remote logging town, working with math and science teachers on content-area reading and vocabulary instruction—topics they did not want to teach. I did my best, spending time collecting tree core samples and touring timber mills; I wrote an un-publishable final report (service grants seldom lead to publications, I later learned) and realized afterward I had missed nine weekends of life with friends and family. The grant award is a single line on my CV, at high cost.

3   Inadequacy

Over my years along the pathway to tenure, pressures and the persistent work imbalance led me to feel an ever-expanding sense of inadequacy. No matter what I did, I was convinced it would not be enough. I asked myself, How might I get more manuscripts published? If I apply myself and work harder, might I get another grant? A larger one? A multi-year research grant? How do my peers from other institutions manage to publish more than I do, while maintaining a cheerful attitude and networking with researchers all across the country?

The Viper likely sensed my growing thoughts of inadequacy and feelings of failure. She offered to help secure an internal technology grant, and I, desperate to achieve more, foolishly said yes. Any momentary elation over receiving an award vanished when I realized I was not on equal footing with the Viper on this project. Deeming herself the expert on all things technology, she seized control of the project. "I've been working in educational technology for years, especially mobile technology as a way to reach underrepresented communities. I don't think you know anything about that." The Viper did the research and creative work, and I ended up installing software updates on 40 mobile devices, one at a time. She also took all of the mobile technology home after the project ended, so that nobody else would be able to use it for any purpose she wasn't part of. I cautiously raised this issue with the dean, believing that the equipment belonged to the university and not to her individually; the dean agreed but did not want to intervene and provoke the Viper's maniacal wrath.

Even though I spent huge amounts of time on course development, teaching and advising, feelings of inadequacy filtered into that part of my work, too. In my school, students can choose their own advisor; not wanting to be picked on by the bitter colleague or ignored by the inattentive benevolent colleague, a large number of students chose the faculty member who was available and eager to please—me. At one point I had 23 graduate student advisees, while the Viper and two other colleagues, together, had nine. The school had no mechanism for faculty to say no to new advisees. I could not find enough time to advise each of them sufficiently and so I felt I was failing them, too.

My sense of inadequacy in teaching came from course evaluations. My mentor and colleague expressed anguish at the end of one semester for getting a combined student course evaluation score of 3.8 out of 5. "I've never gotten such a low score in my whole career. I normally get at least a 4.8 or higher!" I had never gotten a 4.8. What was I doing wrong? Was I failing my students as well as my scholarship? When I send in my tenure file, will my senior colleagues see my student course evaluation scores and shake their heads in dismay? Clearly I wasn't doing enough or working enough, so I tried harder. Every day. For almost six years, until I turned in my tenure file with decent course evaluation scores, several grants and a reasonable number of publications.

4   Attitude

Once I turned in my tenure file I did experience a gradual change of attitude and all the emotions that come along on such a stressful and arduous journey. First I felt a sense of profound relief, followed immediately by fear—after all, the Viper was on my promotion and tenure committee. Her unpredictability and moments of random wrath petrified me, so I remained terrified until, months later, I received notice of my successful tenure and promotion.

Fear was mixed with gratitude during these months, as I came to appreciate several senior colleagues (including Grace) who went to battle for me and neutralized the negative maniacal critiques and actions of the Viper. Outnumbered and outvoted, all she could do was seethe and plot petty schemes to make my tenured life miserable, which she did until her recent retirement. Nobody bothered to throw her a farewell party, although she had been at our institution for almost 30 years. I wondered, what might have happened if I had been in a school with three bitter senior colleagues and one benevolent one, rather than the other way around? I shudder to think about it.

Immediately after receiving tenure I went on sabbatical for a year with high hopes of resetting my work/life balance to make the next 20 years sustainable, positive and interesting. I tried, but the following year I was appointed to leadership positions for a number of years. In a small school with retiring senior colleagues and newly hired junior colleagues, I found I could no more say "no" as an associate professor than I could as an assistant, although the reasons were different.

Looking back across this journey to tenure, it seems that once we arrive we either become benevolent or bitter. Do I manage a better work/life balance, find my teaching stride and a research niche, and be a benevolent colleague like Grace, or do I stay off kilter and miserable like the Viper, spreading bitterness in every meeting and class session? Assistant and Associate are both nine-letter words, but what they represent are worlds apart. Shifting into the new title and role of associate (tenured) professor was a positive experience for me overall, as I realized I was ultimately free to pursue the scholarship I found interesting. It wasn't a publish-or-perish choice anymore; I hadn't perished, so now I could choose. I'm not sure if this has made me a benevolent colleague, but it certainly has kept me from becoming bitter. I say no to service work, but judiciously. I look out for and try to protect my new junior colleagues from too much service work. I choose research projects carefully, focusing on what interests me most. I take weekends off—all of them! I will go up for full professor soon, but the difference is that I get to choose when, based on my own sense of readiness. That makes all the difference. It will be my decision, not the hourglass trickling sand irreversibly, the way it did on the pathway to tenure.

Perhaps the pathway to tenure could be different, more supportive and less arduous, making the outcome more likely to be benevolence rather than bitterness. I wonder, is six years enough time to prove worthiness? Are junior faculty scholarship activities sufficiently supported by university structures? Can junior faculty's time be protected, limiting their service load for work that is highly time-consuming yet counts for little on a CV? It seems that universities have no difficulty in demanding and expecting high amounts of work and effort to achieve tenure. The true difficulty lies in actually supporting junior faculty to succeed in their teaching and scholarship so that they grow through the process in a positive and supported way, emerging from their pre-tenure chrysalis of panic as benevolent butterflies rather than bitter worms.

CHAPTER 16

Observations from a Non-Academic on Academic Life

Ken Robertson

We met about three months before he defended his dissertation. One might say that it was not a likely recipe for success in terms of starting a new relationship. While I had recently left a depressing job for a new one as Construction Project Manager, he was feverishly putting the final touches on his dissertation. Only fellow academics (or their significant others) can understand what those last weeks are like before defending the culmination of years of research and hard work. In those early days of our relationship, our only opportunity to meet was when he would come into the city to see his advisor and we'd be able to work in a quick dinner.

As an ABD (All But Dissertation), he had already accepted a tenure-track position at the University of Washington. I later learned that it is not common for degree-granting institutions to warmly welcome their own newly minted PhD graduates with open arms, which seems rather like shoving the baby bird from the nest. I had always thought that years of academic study were a kind of litmus test, which, if passed, would lead to employment and future success at their department. Wrong! Most commonly, you have to apply elsewhere to find gainful employment and you would be wise to have a back-up plan. So, having survived graduate school and gotten a PhD, you are immediately turned out to swim with the sharks in a very competitive environment. Tony had already been called to interviews across the country, but his first was with his university and they offered him a tenure-track position. Having a bird in the hand, it seemed wise to accept. The interview and his choice to accept occurred before we met, so as much as I like to think I'm a pretty good catch, I can't take credit for being the reason he stayed in Seattle.

The first year or so of dating we shuttled between my small city apartment and his larger suburban one near campus. The benefit of my apartment: it was close to all the fun (and distractions) a city can offer. Benefits of his? He could walk to campus in 10 minutes and owned an Asian shorthair cat that would curl up on his lap as he typed out his dissertation. Tony never stayed overnight in the city the day before he taught a class. He needed that evening and next day to prepare. Like many people, my thoughts of academic life were that professors had a pretty good gig. You work hard to get there, but once you get your job and tenure you can coast. Summers are free for "research" trips and time spent reading books on the beach. Over the course of his early years in academia, I learned that none of those assumptions was remotely true. Achieving tenure would become the first big academic mountain we'd need to climb. I say "we" not because I am an excellent research assistant or typist, but because as partner I found myself in a supporting role. I literally had no idea what I had signed on for. Achieving tenure is a much more arduous and capricious prize to seize than most non-academics perceive. I had assumed that once you have that PhD in hand, you have a clear path to success, with all the support of your university. Although a PhD is definitely a milestone (some might call it a mill stone), it really is just a toehold for the next six years of arduously pushing the rock up the hill like a poor academic Sisyphus to achieve the nirvana that is tenure.

Teaching in and of itself, along with all of its ancillary duties, is a full time job. As a young academic, you somehow still need to find the time to conduct research, publish your work, provide service to your school by participating in various committees and review panels, and still show up at conferences in your field to present your research. Oh, and if you could please, why don't you write a few grant proposals and bring in some dollars for your school and university. I was incredulous that typically 50% of grant funds are held by the university as "overhead cost." It's kind of like doing well at your job and as a reward they give you a 50% pay cut. While there are a wide range of salaries for academics, you don't go into it for the money. University compensation seems grossly out of balance with expectations and makes me wonder if the tenure process is really good for academia in the long term. To me it seems that the playing field is not level for all players. If you are a single parent, for example, how do you accomplish tenure and still have a family life?

As I learned these truths of academic life, I pondered how our new relationship would find space to grow and thrive. Even in the best of circumstances, relationships are hard work and I wondered if there would still be time for discovery and fun? How do you provide support for someone who needs you but also needs you to give them space to get through the epic volume of work laid out before them? As Tony wrote and wrote and wrote, I would occupy myself with other things. Sometimes that meant going to a movie on my own or planning a social event he might not be able to participate in. The more he wrote, the more I felt like it would never stop. It was as if he was working on an endless term paper—one that with a little bit of luck he might be done with in six years. In my career I oversee development and design for large senior housing projects around the US, and I could not imagine sitting down and working on the same project for that long of an extended time frame, refining the details over and over again. In my management of architects and interior designers, I often get to a point where I tell them "Pencils down," meaning this is as good as it's going to get, let's move on to the next steps of the project and get it built. My project work has a distinct beginning and end. You typically work as a team and share the experience with others. You gain experience from doing it, but you also get to move on to the next project and often with a new team of colleagues.

There were many Saturdays and Sundays Tony spent working. We would try and save one of the weekend days for something fun that we could do together. A day trip or a hike, dinner and a movie. Somehow his demanding academic pace had to be reconciled with our relationship. The scale often tipped toward academia, but to his credit, he managed to keep me in the picture. As a partner of an academic, I have learned that at times you must draw on a deep well of patience and understanding. I certainly failed at times, but the more our relationship grew, I understood that I had a role to play as well. To support, to listen and to occasionally make myself scarce when he needed time for focused work and reflection.

I travel a great deal for my career and routinely use my corporate credit card for business travel, hotels and meals with clients. In academia there is no such thing as an expense account, let alone any kind of reasonable budget to support your work. You are expected to attend and participate in conferences all across the country on a travel budget that usually only covers airfare and accommodation for one such event per year. The expense of any additional conferences is laid at the feet of young academics to absorb from their already less than stellar annual salaries. When I asked Tony about this, he said it was the nature of things at universities–an expectation without financial support. I thought that not much business would be conducted in this world if employers did not cover expenses. If it's the expectation of your employer that you need to travel as a condition of your employment as well as for the success of the business, then it stands to reason that your employer would be taking care of this cost. Not so in academia. For young academics, who often might be shouldering student debt, this seems doubly unfair.

Over the years, I have joined Tony at various faculty social events. As a spouse of an academic, I can tell you that the occasional social gatherings are a bit awkward for someone like me who is not able to connect on an academic level. I think of these as "putting all the smart people together in a room." It's not that people aren't social, but with such infrequent gatherings, there is awkwardness. Talking about non-academic topics is a bit challenging in these group settings. I think if you are an academic who toils away on your own for the most part, it can be daunting to be in social interaction with your peers.

Professionally, when you put a group of people with a high level of intelligence in the same room, you will find that they generally possess very differing conceptual framework filters, and thus conflicts can occur and you end up with fractious moments. I have watched with fascination and some degree of horror as common workplace problems or squabbles can quickly turn into something otherworldly. Being correct in your work and research is vital for an academic.

Much of the conflict I have observed does not come from the work or research but rather from the endless administrative tasks and committee work. How do you approach a problem? How do you structure a program? What kinds of support are necessary for students? I have often observed manipulation on a grand scale among academics. Every job has office politics, but for an academic they seem to evolve in a way that is completely foreign to me. In my professional life, people come and go. Some you like, some you don't. If you disagree with someone or their approach to a problem, hopefully you can negotiate a path forward to some kind of resolution. Occasionally you have a boss you don't like and your choice is to either work out your differences, put up with it or quit. The private sector isn't a workers' paradise, but generally speaking you find like-minded colleagues and with a little luck they can become your friends, too.

In academic life, you find colleagues with whom you might be able to collaborate on research, or commiserate over committee work, but the stakes are high. There is a competitive dynamic among junior faculty. The overarching goal is to achieve tenure and the pathway is not always clear on how to get there. Do you need to curry favor with an older, more experienced faculty member? Should you volunteer more of your precious time to support an issue or cause they are championing, or are you merely someone on whom more work can be off-loaded? Faculty meetings can be contentious and problems and resentments can build up over time. And with typically infrequent injections of fresh talent, and sometimes long stretches between meetings with colleagues due to busy schedules, there often is not enough time to build good working relationships. With effort, good relationships can develop, but it is often not the natural course of things. Relationship-building that might take weeks or months to achieve in private sector work environments might take years in academia, if ever. You really have to work at it.

There is no playbook on how to achieve tenure but make no mistake that there is a game to be played. That may sound sinister, but without the kindly guidance of a true colleague or mentor, it can be a very long six years. As I watched my spouse toil away for six years, I never really had any doubt that he would achieve tenure. As for his endless term paper, he did indeed finish it. Tenure was not a gift, but rather earned by hard work and sacrifice. I now know what it takes to achieve this and I'm proud of his efforts.

Currently, our next destination on this journey is promotion to full professor. He is almost there and I have no doubt that he'll make it. He possesses a drive and ambition that most private sector employers would love to harness. And I'm getting better at knowing when to push and pull the levers of support when needed. I also know when it's a good time to go see a movie on my own. Balance, effort and striving to be better are not just academic pursuits, they are also really great relationship fundamentals.

CHAPTER 17

Harassment and Abuse of Power from a Global Perspective

Or the Importance of a Conversation

Anonymous 7

This essay tells highly personal stories, which nevertheless convey uncomfortable recurring motifs, as well as possible blind spots—things we did not know yet. As we do know, however, many people in worldwide academia—students, scholars and administrative staff of all genders—fall victim to abuse of power or harassment at some point in their academic journey. Most of the problems can ultimately be traced back to a basic pattern, in which those with power abuse those who are "weaker"—who lack resources and backing by peers, institutional power or stable employment. But this pattern comes in many guises. Some people face verbal or physical harassment. Others have to watch their work being plagiarized or are forced to do things they do not want to do. There is no single, unified narrative.

While working in an academic institution in a country where I was not born or educated, I gradually became aware that the problems of abuse of power and intimidation are often culturally determined, at least to some extent. Sometimes it was even explained to me: *It's just part of the culture and you just have to adapt.* It convinced me that awareness of cultural aspects is crucial for a better understanding of the nature and scope of harassment and abuse of power. In this essay, I do not just reflect on my own experiences, but also on those of others, with the aim of learning from the experiences and considerations of people from different cultures than mine.[1] What can we learn from each other by telling our personal and often painful stories, and how could an awareness of the cultural dimension of abuse in the academic world help us process our own experiences? What is the cultural dimension of our particular experiences, and what is more general? And what does the global nature of abuse and harassment imply for the responsibility of academics towards the worldwide academic community?

1   Consolation and New Insights

It was not easy to find the right form for this essay. I started over at least three times, if not more. Every time I tried to write down the events that upset me as a PhD student, they seemed so trivial that I wondered exactly what had happened, and if my experiences actually qualified as forms of intimidation and abuse of power. At the same time, these memories evoked strong emotions, which were difficult to put into words.

The breakthrough came when a colleague shared her experiences with me from the time she worked at a university in Northwestern Europe.[2] Just like me, she was a foreigner and educated in a country that, although it was "Western," was very different from her new homeland. One of the things she noticed was a different attitude towards hierarchy. She told me,

> I felt that hierarchies of rank were more closely adhered to in comparison with the bulk of my experience in my home country [the US], which places great emphasis on independence and individual choice. In many cases, it is considered bullying to pull rank on someone or to force or intimidate a person into doing something they have the option of not doing. It took me some time to realize this aspect of my new culture, which I would consider falling under more serious abuse of power when faculty make unreasonable demands in caustic and insulting ways of those with lower rank—whether administrative staff, grad students or post-docs.

My colleague's words helped me to formulate my own experiences. I realized that what she described was exactly what had upset me early on in my academic career. I found it very difficult to process these events back then, not least because they were sometimes covered up by "higher"-ranked people such as my supervisors, or colleagues who should have protected me, such as confidential advisors, and ombudsmen. It was immensely comforting to hear my colleague say years later that she had faced similar problems. "This is not an aspect of the culture prominently displayed or vocalized, even though it is a major source of anxiety and depression among employees which continually leads to massive burnout and high turnover rates." Apparently, my experiences were not as trivial as they had seemed. They had been experienced by more people than just me.

My colleague also confirmed what I already sensed, namely that the culture of my new homeland was more hierarchical than that of other countries. I had grown up and gone to school in a country where there was little distance between teacher and student. They could communicate and work together on an equal footing more easily than in my new home country. In the latter, however, it was more acceptable that people with a "higher" position would delegate certain tasks to lower-ranked people, often without much possibility to refuse the request. My native colleagues had fewer difficulties than I did in accepting these requests, as they considered them part of the culture in which they were raised. It made me aware of the fact that the ways in which power relations are constructed and perceived by people are culturally determined. I also realized that there must be a strong cultural dimension to the problems of abuse of power and intimidation in academia.

2   No Single Narratives

One of my most formative and positive experiences as a PhD student was when I was invited to participate in a summer school for PhD students, on a topic that was very close to that of my dissertation. Apart from the fact that I gained a lot of substantial knowledge on which I am still building in my current research, it was an unforgettable experience on a human level.

Normally, at academic events branded as "international," you will mostly meet scholars from the rich, privileged (and therefore highly-ranked) universities of the "West." However, the organizers had deliberately chosen to invite a mix of students from different cultural backgrounds. I remember students from Venezuela, Georgia, Sweden, Poland, Belgium, France, Cuba and Syria (the latter two making jokes about having fled from there by boat, a joke few others would be in the position to make). The summer school was free of charge, in contrast with other international academic events, which are usually quite expensive and therefore out of reach for many scholars—especially the younger ones from less-privileged institutions. Most summer school students had only minimal financial scholarships—if any—and probably would not have been able to afford the summer school had it not been free. Extra scholarships were awarded to those who could not pay the travel expenses.

This experience reminded me of the fact that there is much financial inequality in the academic world, depending on the wealth of one's institution and/or home country. I also learned that if you are in the privileged position to have sufficient financial resources, you can actively do something to reduce that inequality, for example, by selecting and paying for people who normally do not have the resources to participate in international events. Scholars can make a difference in global academia by using their funds intentionally.

I also became aware of certain blind spots in my own thinking about the academic world. Because we often know only our own story and do not get in touch with academics from other cultures, we do not realize—or do not real- ize enough—that there are other stories as well, especially when it comes to power relations within the academy. If I had not attended this summer school and talked to scholars from other cultures, I might have believed that abuse of power was mainly something between a professor and student, or at least between academics that are not on the same rung of the academic ladder. I would not have realized that abuse of power can also result from the unequal division of resources and asymmetrical relationships between wealthy and less-wealthy academic institutions in different parts of the world.

3   Intercultural Conversations

While wrestling with this essay, I stumbled upon Hans-Georg Gadamer's idea of the fusion of horizons. According to Gadamer's *Truth and Method*, "Under- standing is always the process of a fusion of these horizons supposedly existing for themselves" (2004, p. 306). I was familiar with Gadamer's idea from my phi- losophy classes as an undergraduate, in which it was discussed as part of the question of how to obtain knowledge. I did not know that this model also deals with intercultural communication. According to Gadamer, in order to under- stand the other, we have to demonstrate a willingness to listen to what the other has to say. One has to learn to "look beyond what is close at hand—not in order to look away from it but to see it better, within in a larger whole and in truer proportion" (p. 305). In this conversation with the other, one's earlier expectations are fused with the new experiences and simultaneously super- seded by a new horizon of understanding.

It occurred to me that Gadamer's detached way of looking at things, beyond the matter close at hand, might be a good way to give place to my personal and painful experiences of harassment and abuse of power, and to gain more insight into the nature of these problems in academia. What was general, and what was culturally specific? I also realized that Gadamer's call to open up and listen to the other was probably the only way to detect blind spots in my own thinking and to better know what my responsibilities are towards my col- leagues in the academic world.

Over the past few months, I have spoken with academics from different parts of the world whom I've met during my, at this point, relatively short jour- ney through the academy. I spoke with D., a lecturer from the United States, with R., an assistant professor from Mexico, and with G., a lecturer from India. I deeply admire their courage and willingness to share their stories with me and am grateful for all the things I learned from them. Here I would like to share some of the recurring elements I discerned in the stories of my international conversation partners, as well as some of the blind spots I had, as a scholar trained and later employed at one of the many wealthy, privileged universities in Northwestern Europe.

4   Blind Spots

One of my blind spots was due simply to the fact that the form of power abuse did not originate in my own culture. This is the problem of caste discrimination in India, pointed out by my colleague G. from India. Caste discrimination is a serious obstacle to attaining a PhD position, she says. "Candidates are selected based on their caste affiliations, which are clearly identifiable through their surnames. The practice continues in the process of appointment of supervisors." It also affects the evaluation of the research of PhD students. "Often a high caste professor is appointed as the supervisor for the student from a similar background and a professor from a lower caste background is appointed to advise a student from lower castes. This creates much inequality, especially since students from the lower castes are evaluated by teachers from higher castes on their research presentations, oral exams and thesis defenses."

Before my conversation with G., I had never thought about the implications of the caste system for academic life in India. If you would have asked me, I would have supposed that it would not have affected academic life that much, trusting that humanities scholars in India would be more sensitive to such issues of discrimination. Some undoubtedly are, and are perhaps fighting these problems. Others may have blind spots, just like me.

Other blind spots had to do with problems of which I was vaguely aware, but which I had not given much further thought. An example is the abuse of power arising from institutional discrimination, something which is certainly present in Europe, too, although it is not talked about much. My Mexican colleague R. works at an institution she defines as "outside the core of the academic world defined by the big universities and international rankings," a "renowned but low-resourced institution compared to others in and beyond Mexico." The institution is seen as peripheral to other universities in the Spanish-speaking realm.

The perceived "lower" status of R.'s university has a direct impact on her access to the academic world. "Alterity is a critical issue in this context," she observes. "Decisions such as acceptance of an abstract for a conference, or invited lectures, are many times guided by tacit prejudices about the other." It leaves her in a "vulnerable position," she says, not least because she does not have the institutional resources to fight back, but only her own personal ones. As R. seems to suggest by "tacit prejudices," the discrimination is at least partly the result of the fact that scholars—especially those from wealthier and higher-ranked institutions, who are in charge of most of the international academic events and communication channels—are guided by certain presuppositions about which they may not even be aware, and about which they never really talk to another.

R.'s story makes it clear that such asymmetric inter-institutional power relations also reinforce forms of abuse in academia. She herself became the victim of plagiarism and sloppy source referencing. R. discovered that parts of her research—both central ideas and previous publications, and newly presented sources—had been used by scholars from higher-ranked universities in Mexico and other Spanish-speaking countries who even copied parts of her writings, most often without reference to her work. Having discovered this, she wrote to the editors of the publication and pointed out to them the similarities between the texts in question. The editors expressed concern, but evaded the issue. R.'s complaint was essentially dismissed.

R. felt that her concerns and complaints were not taken seriously, and that her case had suffered from the fact that she did not have the affiliation and contacts that the other scholar could have had. Instances of plagiarism and sloppy citation, seemingly informed by asymmetric power relations, are usually kept under the radar. However, they invoke the question of to what extent they are part of a much bigger problem in which scholars use their position at the expense of scholars in more vulnerable positions.

I discovered more easily-overlooked examples of intimidation and abuse of power in academia. G. tells about how it was made impossible for her to get a PhD position because she had the "wrong" political views. "Soon after I completed my master's degree, there was an opening for a temporary teaching position for which I applied. The interviewer mentioned that although I was the most qualified candidate, they would not offer me the position. The underlying reason was well-known to all the candidates—a difference of political opinion. The faculty were strong supporters of the right wing and I wasn't." G. learned "to maintain a safe distance between professors of a different opinion, religion or caste, and not to openly state her opinion."

Such occurrences, in which academics are put in a vulnerable position or abused because of their personal views or beliefs, also occur at European universities. I remember how a colleague once asked me not to tell anyone that he was a Christian, because he was afraid that he would be taken less seriously and bullied. There seems to be a tendency among scholars not to be open about their personal convictions, especially when they are different from what is considered mainstream at a certain faculty or university. This situation is widely accepted and often remains unquestioned. It is one of the blind spots in the discourse about abuse of power and intimidation at Western European universities.

5   Recurring Elements and Trends

From my conversations it also became clear that in addition to blind spots—which sometimes have to do with culture-specific dimensions of harassment and abuse of power—there are general elements that keep recurring in different cultures. Some are at the root of abuse of power and intimidation; others rather aggravate the problems.

One of these recurring elements is what D. calls a "bottom-line approach to higher education" in the US. She means that universities are expected to make money from their academic activities, "to turn a profit, turning students into customers, and faculty into disposable cogs in a machine." Many of these detrimental developments are also threatening the European academic world, D. feels, where "output is greatly emphasized, as if research institutions are factories, sacrificing quality in favor of quantity." The bottom-line approach leads to inequality and discrimination, D. says. "Hiring committees tend to select internally favored candidates or only seek graduates of elite institutions or male, white candidates of European descent. Tenure committees demand more of women and women of color than they do of their white male counterparts of European descent. And temporary (adjunct) positions are steadily replacing full-time positions."

One of the most striking recurring elements is the difficulty victims experience in raising issues of abuse in academia and fighting against it. "Being a woman in academia," R. says, "I have experienced and witnessed the difficulties of fighting against plagiarism when you appeal to male committees at more powerful institutions that have to resolve your case but seem more interested in defending their journals, colleagues or institutions. No fair play at all and nearly no institutional resources to help you." D. suggests that this is an institutionalized problem. "Sexual harassment and intimidation of faculty of lower rank and students are often kept secret, with the abuser—sometimes serial abusers—with prominent standing in the scholarly community protected."

The fear of speaking out can be reinforced by the cultural context. In India, G. notes, "Most often incidences [of abuse] do not come to light for fear that the student will lose all that he/she has worked for. The common reason for all these instances in India is caste, religious or political difference, sense of hierarchy and seniority, and sometimes personal enmity or disagreement. These cases are not only local, as the instances mentioned above come from across the country. The abuse of power based on religion or caste is mostly seen as a part of culture, rarely do people speak or raise a voice against it." I had the same experience in my own country, where I heard from both undergraduate and postgraduate students that they did not dare report certain abusive behaviors of their professors (verbal intimidation, the making of unreasonable requests). On the one hand, this was out of fear that it would harm their careers, on the other hand, out of the conviction that a complaint would not matter anyway, because the abuse was part of the culture.

6   Broadened Horizon

What did I gain from these conversations with colleagues around the world? They helped me come to terms with my own experiences, find words for them and realize that they were not trivial but *did* matter, because others had similar experiences. I learned that there is no single story but many, even if the basic pattern is usually the same, involving the abuse of the more vulnerable by a more powerful person. I also broadened my own horizon of understanding, detecting blind spots in my own thinking, especially when it comes to expectations, habits and social structures at the base of abuse of power and harassment in particular cultures—India's caste system, for instance, or the unequal power relations between institutions within a country, or among countries. Such elements, which are usually culturally specific, easily escape the attention of people who do not belong to the given culture. Sometimes they contribute to keeping asymmetrical power relations and all their consecutive problems of abuse and intimidation intact.

It also confirmed for me that there are elements and trends recurring in stories of abuse around the globe. Such recurring patterns may help to make this essay relevant to people from areas that go unmentioned here, such as Eurasia, Africa and Oceania. The idea that we share a story is a relief—*I'm not the only one* who had to deal with verbal intimidation by supervisors, who felt forced by higher-ranked colleagues into uncomfortable situations and was confronted with the grey zone of plagiarism by a close colleague. But the fact that there is something like a shared story is also hugely alarming. For if we are aware that there is a problem with abuse in academia which is even global, why does the problem continue? Another essay is probably needed to answer this question, even if it is clear that unequal power relationships within and between institutions and countries play a crucial role.

The conversations with my international colleagues made me realize that abuse in academia is indeed a global problem that requires a global approach. There are many ways to raise awareness and contribute to a solution: expanding our networks with colleagues in more vulnerable situations or from disadvantaged institutions and countries; inviting them to join our academic events, give lectures or submit papers to our books and journals; and financially supporting colleagues who lack the means to participate in international academic events. I think scholars working in more privileged and wealthy environments have a particular responsibility to use their resources and influence in ways that reduce the problem of inequality, which is often at the root of harassment and abuse of power.

Moreover, as I learned while writing this essay, it helps to intentionally engage in conversations with scholars from around the globe in order to become more aware of the scope of the problems of power abuse and harassment in academia. We can detect our shared stories, our own blind spots and our tacit assumptions only if we open up to the other person, engage in real and honest conversation, and listen to their experiences.

7 My Struggle

If a conversation is so important to understand the other person, should we talk to our abusers? The answer will be different for everyone. Some people will never want to see their abuser again, because the offense was too grave or the memory too raw. Others have the courage to expose wrongdoings, which is a very tough thing to do. Still others like me do not dare to enter into a conversation or name wrongdoers for fear of further damage.

Exposure is crucial to break the silence surrounding the abuse and disclose the truth. One of the things I struggled with while writing this essay was whether I should put my own name on it. I did not have the courage, being afraid that it would affect my career, which I have worked so hard for. At the same time, it seemed unfair to me to present my side of the story without giving my colleagues the possibility of responding. By this I do not mean that I would like to cover things up or defend my offenders. But we all have our own stories of what happened, and they are inevitably impacted by the fact that we originate from different cultures. I think the truth only comes to light if we open up to another in a real and honest conversation, in which we explain how we experienced things, and, if possible, try to bring each other's horizons somewhat closer.

But what if, like me, you do not dare have such a conversation, or if it is simply impossible? I learned a lot from the book *Free of Charge* (2005), by the Croatian-American theologian Miroslav Volf, whose thinking about dialogue, exposure and forgiveness was directly informed by the fact that he grew up in a family belonging to the Protestant-Christian minority in former Yugoslavia, at a time when the country was torn by deep ethnic and religious tensions. Volf suggests that exposure is not necessarily about disclosing the culprit, but the deeds. He refers to William Shakespeare's play "Measure for Measure," which tells about Claudio, who is sentenced to death for getting his beloved pregnant. Claudio's sister Isabella asks the judge to show mercy and to spare her brother's life. She says,

> I have a brother is condemn'd to die.
> I do beseech you let it be his fault,
> And not my brother.
> (Shakespeare, quoted in Volf, 2005, p. 141)

Volf notes the following about the passage: "To be just is to condemn the fault, and, because of the fault, to condemn the doer as well. To forgive is to condemn the fault but to spare the doer" (p. 141). Elsewhere, Volf states that forgiveness entails two things: first, "to name the wrongdoing and to condemn it" (p. 129); and second, "to give the wrongdoers the gift of not counting the wrongdoing against them" (p. 130). One can see why exposure and forgiveness should go together. On the one hand, mere forgiveness of the offender without identifying the wrongdoing can easily result in a situation in which the wrong is covered up and the potentially abusive situation perpetuated (something that happens all too often in academia). On the other hand, mere exposure of the fault without forgiveness can lead to bitterness and resentment (something that is often seen in academia, too).

Volf helped me to come to terms with my own story of intimidation and abuse in academia, suggesting that it is also okay to expose faults without naming the wrongdoer. With this in mind, I have tried to keep a distance, leaving the culprits for what they are, while exposing some general trends in abuse and harassment in academia and blind spots in mine (and possibly others') thinking about the problems. Sometimes it is enough just to trace the contours of what went wrong without publicly condemning individual perpetrators and counting wrongdoings against them, in the hope that it opens up the space for a *real* conversation in which we can better find each other.

Notes

1   My leading questions were inspired by Regulska (2018). Many of the problems exposed by the #MeToo movement as underlying causes of sexual harassment are similar to those underlying abuse and intimidation in academia in general.

2   I have tried to give as faithful a representation as possible of what colleagues wanted to share
    with me verbally and on paper, quoting their words verbatim. Moreover, I have submitted
    this essay to them for approval. Still, it is ultimately mainly the expression of my own position
    on the problem of harassment and abuse of power in academia.

References

Gadamar, H.-G. (2004). *Truth and method* (2nd ed., J. Weinsheimer & D. G. Marshall,
    Trans.). Continuum.

Regulska, J. (2018). The #MeToo movement as a global learning moment. *International
    Higher Education, 94*(5), 5–6. https://www.researchgate.net/publication/
    325701024_The_MeToo_Movement_as_a_Global_Learning_Moment

Volf, M. (2005). *Free of charge: Giving and forgiving in a culture stripped of grace*. Grand
    Rapids.

CHAPTER 18

What My Younger Self Would Have Said, Had She Spoken up, and How My Present Self Would Have Replied

Ingela Nilsson

"There was this seminar the other day and I really didn't get anything, or at least close to nothing. Everyone else seemed to understand, nodding and smiling and laughing, so I did what I always do: mimicked them, feeling stupid on the inside while laughing along on the outside. Some part of me knows this is wrong, but I've been doing it for so long it's too late to admit I don't quite belong. Otherwise people would realize that I don't know all these terms they're using, that I haven't read all those books they refer to in passing as if everyone had read everything. But above all, I don't want to expose myself by asking a wrong or stupid question. They would laugh, and even if I could laugh along, my embarrassment might shine through and it would all be over."

"What would be over?"

"Eh … this! Being part of this world, learning things, having coffee, going for drinks, being at university, you know. I like it here, it's very different from anything I ever knew, and I've made friends. In fact, they are my best friends—we do everything together, from morning to late at night."

"But look, if you cannot tell them you don't understand something, are they really your friends? Do they really know you? Aren't they just a bunch of guys who enjoy having a young woman in their circle?"

"What a mean thing to say! Of course they know me, they know who I am now: one of them. And what's wrong with being the only girl anyhow? In fact, it makes me feel special, I get a lot of attention. And I'm not some dumb chick, you know! I'm a cool girl, one of the guys, they respect me for that and treat me the same way they treat each other."

"Seriously: you cannot believe that. You're like a mascot to them, they think you're cute. And how can you claim you're just one of the guys? Did any of them speak up when you filed a complaint against that professor with the sexist translation exercises? Did any of them stand up for you? No, they did not. They are using you as a front figure when they dislike something, you get to be the angry girl who takes the fire and the blame. You will see, that's how it works."

"What a bitch you are, just because you can't remember what it's like to be young—I bet you're just jealous, wishing you were in my place. They've actually been really supportive."

"Like when they wrote that poem about your breasts? Or left you alone late at night with that guy trying to seduce you? Look, I don't doubt their affection for you, but I bet most of them are just as scared as you are of looking stupid or making a mistake. You become an alibi, a kind of reflection of what they don't have the guts to be."

"You're so mean, I never want to speak to you again."

"That's fine, we will never have this conversation anyhow. I just hope you won't get too hurt and give up your integrity, it's the last thing we can afford to lose."

"I'll be fine, if you just get out of my head."

CHAPTER 19

The Ghosts of Academia

Veronika Muchitsch

I am haunted by a particular kind of ghosts.

At times, they materialize in the subtle sting of mistrust upon new encounters. At others, they form a knot in my gut, heavy with anger and disenchantment. They embody the specific kind of pain caused by the ruptures between feminist theory and proclamations, and lived feminist practice in academia.

I have struggled with following this perspective in this contribution. Many of these specters echo encounters with scholars, who are self-proclaimed feminists and feminist theorists, whose work I had admired, and still admire. Others formed within institutional contexts that off-handedly declare commitment to feminist politics, and, most excruciatingly, within scholarly networks, whose pronounced purpose it is to scrutinize and fight intersecting forms of subjugation including those along lines of gender, sexuality, class, race and ethnicity.

I have struggled, as well, because giving voice to my experiences would risk diverting attention from other, more explicitly misogynist, displays of abuse of power. And because pointing to these problems threatened to cancel out the experiences of feminist companionship and support that have carried me through my early career in academia.

But my ghosts would not dissolve. They expanded and multiplied with time, with reflection.

So, I knew I needed to paint their shadows on these pages.

© VERONIKA MUCHITSCH, 2022 | DOI:10.1163/9789004521025_019

Professors become mentors

mentoring turns to grooming

turns to gaslighting

Theoretical critiques of neoliberalism

actions that perpetuate precarious

existences within academia

Established scholars

crushing junior colleagues' work

and trust and confidence

Normative and exclusionary practices

within feminist spaces

Institutional cultures of silence

and shame surrounding

misconduct and harassment

CHAPTER 20

The Unbearable Shame of Crying at Work

Anonymous 8

Like many academics, I have over the years experienced various situations of abuse and harassment. I developed coping strategies that helped me to move on, but they were not necessarily positive for me. I believe that opportunities to share and reflect on experiences of abusive situations provide one of the most constructive ways to find healthy strategies to counteract this type of behavior.

I was spared during my first semesters in academia. Apart from a few incidents of wandering hands at department parties, most lecturers treated me with respect. I was completely unprepared, however, for my first encounter with my future supervisor in France. I was excited to be there, but when I went to see her after class, her gaze remained trained on the wall behind me, signaling clearly my inferiority and insignificance as she coldly explained that she would not meet with me until next year, and only if I passed my master exams. She also advised me that on days when students came out of her office crying, it was better to postpone the appointment. During my five years as her graduate student, there were many such days when I consciously avoided her out of fear of bursting into tears in front of her and everyone else. All her students feared committing faux pas in her presence, as she could be mean enough even on a good day.

This was the history of the department. Her predecessor had made her suffer tremendously for years and years as a lecturer and it was only by playing power games that she had finally attained this position. She was not a particularly brilliant or successful researcher, but she was a ruthless strategist who held the entire department in thrall to her persona.

She was not ready to open up to anyone at that time. Later on, during the long periods of illness that finally led to her death, her attitude changed, and one day soon after I had defended my PhD, she apologized for how she had behaved during my first years as her graduate student.

I was lucky to be able to work on my PhD at an international research institute, although I didn't have a grant and had to work in different projects on the side. It was a vibrant environment with scholars of all ages and nationalities passing through. Being abroad made them more open and accessible than at their home institutions. I was happy and inspired to share ideas with researchers with common interests and with whom scholarly exchange was independent of age or gender. Or at least that's what I thought.

One day I was sitting together with a local colleague on a little bench outside the library of the international institute. He was a senior researcher, but we often sat there together, discussing our research, new publications or interesting buildings. But today was different. The air was thick. He obviously felt it, too, for he was sweating and breathing heavily.

"It's very simple," he said, "you do something for me and I'll do something for you. You can begin by filling in this form and returning it to my post box within a week. Then I'll know and can make arrangements accordingly …"

Who in my position wouldn't want a grant to spend a semester at a prestigious research institute? It would be an ideal opportunity to write my dissertation with a full salary, with access to an amazing library and renowned scholars. But it was not due to my intellectual capacity, research topic or innovative methodology that I would receive this. None of these things were of interest in this exchange of services. Shame, disgust and guilt surfaced in my mind and I could feel the tears burning. But I didn't want anyone to know about this shameful experience, so I kept a straight face. A few days later he reminded me to turn in the grant application. I did so without having filled it out. He pretended it had never happened, but he never, ever discussed research with me again.

In a job interview a couple of years later, I mentioned the situation as an example of how I had dealt with harassment, and I later learned that this had got me the position. It was outside of academia, but it was also an opportunity to finish my PhD without exchanging services with anyone.

When I returned to academia as a postdoctoral researcher, I needed to go on longer research trips to reconnect with the field and my topic. I also reestablished contact with researchers I knew from before, many of whom were close to retirement, but very knowledgeable in the field. One of them had spent all his professional life working on the same period as I specialized in. When I was on a research visit in the city where he lived, he invited me to stay at his house.

"Come and stay at my place," he said. "No reason to take a room at the institute, there are so few. I can introduce you to my networks here and we can discuss your work after hours." I agreed, of course, eagerly.

This was followed by several exciting meetings with interesting colleagues, long days of archival research and long evening talks about the history of the discipline and the current research environment in our field. It was such a pleasure to finally get to know a senior researcher who understood and appreciated my work. There was a wonderful intellectual connection that developed and made me feel more confident about my own value and contributions as a researcher.

One night I was awoken by someone slipping under my covers.

"I can't sleep," he said. "I need to feel the warmth of another human being."

I slipped out of bed, went into the kitchen that smelled of cold tobacco and spent the rest of the night on a plastic chair smoking and staring into the dark, concentrating very hard in order not to cry. The bond of trust and equal dialogue had obviously only existed in my mind. All that was left now was sadness, anger and disappointment. I left early in the morning, before he woke up.

We stayed in touch because his work was intertwined with mine through documents and connections that I could not disregard or avoid without coming across as unprofessional. I remained silent for years, until he passed away.

In the numerous recommendation letters he subsequently wrote for me, one sentence was recurrently used—a person with an extraordinary integrity and loyalty.

The vulnerability to harassment may decrease over the course of a career and with age, but exposure to abuse of power, unclear distribution of (or exclusion from) responsibility and non-transparent decision-making processes are power strategies that can be just as intimidating, confusing and disorienting. The effects of such behavior can be similar to that of gaslighting, when the perpetrator manipulates another person into doubting their perception of reality.

When such a situation recently occurred at my workplace, my reaction was surprisingly different from twenty years ago. Instead of heavy, cold silence and guilt spreading in my mind, I could not stop myself from expressing anger and frustration. As floods of angry tears rushed over my face, I gave voice to my thoughts about the situation. This time I conveyed my opinion to a person mature enough to take the emotional reaction and who was wise enough to allow me the space and time I needed to reformulate my thoughts into something constructive. But I was also confident enough to express my anger and cry without shame, and mature enough to take a step back, analyze the situation and find a solution that was positive for me.

Harassment and abuse, whether emotional or physical, are ways of maintaining power structures. They can also be a source of pleasure for the perpetrator. They are means of controlling or isolating strong individuals who are perceived as a threat, or weaker individuals considered easy prey, denigrating their intellectual capacity and equal rights.

One recurring observation I have made of academia in general, and the humanities in particular, is that students and young researchers are especially vulnerable due to the nature of the field, lack of funding and lack of permanent positions. This situation opens up a space for individuals in power positions to abuse or harass those with less power. Sometimes this behavior seems to be hereditary within a department, following the logic of "my professor/

supervisor did this to me, thus I'm entitled to behave the same way when I attain the same position." Sometimes it is attributed to a certain individual who is so brilliant that no one dares to question their behavior, although it is clearly that of a bully.

The culture of silence and guilt that protects the perpetrators needs to be addressed and dealt with. I know from experience that it is difficult to deal with something like this on your own. In addition, the unbearable shame of crying in an academic environment makes us keep it all to ourselves. It took me two decades before I was confident and mature enough to cry without shame in front of my boss. We need to raise awareness and create possibilities to share experiences and get advice anonymously. Although it may be difficult to eliminate harassment and abuse completely from any workplace, opening spaces where experiences can be shared can strengthen those exposed to it and diminish the personal and professional damage it causes.

CHAPTER 21

Panic Button

Ingela Nilsson

A colleague and former student sent me a draft essay the other week, asking for advice about where to publish it. It was a brilliant text, discussing gendered aspects of translation and the strong, basically corporeal sense of not belonging that women sometimes feel in certain contexts and environments. I was impressed, but also distressed, because the essay contained a personal anecdote from her time as a student. The (male) teacher had written a sentence for translation on the whiteboard and said "This sentence is about you." She was the only female student in the room. "I tried to understand how this sentence, a sentence that commented a woman's body in sexual terms, could be about me. I was not a body? I was a student." The function of this memory was to describe her own discovery of being reduced to a body, being reminded of her flesh. Framed by citations from Christine de Pizan and Simone de Beauvoir, it made for a strong case, but the reason why my heart started beating (in my own body) was that this incident had happened under my watch—at a time when I was responsible for all our undergraduate teaching.

I instantly tried to remember who had been teaching what course back then, in an attempt to identify the person who had done this to her, feeling ashamed and embarrassed that something like this had happened without my ever knowing or noticing. But it was a futile effort, because the time at which this would have happened was not only distant in time but also rather muddled in my memory, due to the kind of situation I had found myself in back then: new at the job and under constant critique from colleagues who wished someone else had been in my place. Was it even possible that she told me or wrote about this in an evaluation and I had simply forgotten? That thought made me even more distressed, reminding me of how easy it is to miss other people's distress when one is feeling unhappy, tired and weak.

Then I remembered an email I had received a few months back from another young woman, a PhD student whom I had met at a few occasions. We had shared some bad experiences of a colleague misbehaving and wrote messages every now and then. In a recent email, she had suggested a remedy for bad behavior in drastic but memorable words:

Increasingly, when talking to friends and colleagues about these experiences, I have found myself wishing that we could install a sizeable red button on each desk in our academic environments, linked to a loud buzzer and a large neon red sign of the word INAPPROPRIATE at the back of the room. This is (though perhaps only half) a joke of course, but I think the idea illustrates the lonely feeling that goes with how often even public inappropriate behavior goes unchallenged. I have even experienced how awkward laughs that ensue from the discomfort of the audience can be perceived (by victim and perpetrator) as encouragement of bad behavior.

A panic button! That is what my student should have had on that occasion some ten years ago! A red button and a neon sign going INAPPROPRIATE! The shame would have been turned away from her and instead bounced back at that teacher, whoever he was. In fact, that email put words to something that had been at the back of my mind for quite some time: the culture of silence that reigns in classrooms and lecture halls, in seminar rooms and lunch rooms, in any kind of academic setting that I have ever known. We see things, we hear things, but we pretend as if they are not there. I don't even think it's out of spite, most of the time; it is rather an inability to cope, an embarrassment or awkwardness, not knowing how to deal with inappropriate behavior. The author of the email had recognized that as she wisely went on:

> Clearly, as a community, we simply don't know how to respond, or rarely have the presence or wherewithal to do so appropriately when these circumstances present themselves (and I recognize this in myself as well). Perhaps it's a good idea, in absence of a red buzzer button, to offer simple ways to speak up, or other things to do, when inappropriate behavior presents itself in a public setting.

Yes, but this is the trick question, isn't it? What other ways to speak up do we have, when there are no panic buttons and when so many are afraid to break the silence? I cannot even count the times that I heard people say "Someone should have stopped him," or "Why didn't anybody tell her?" I've said it myself, too. Spent sleepless nights trying to understand what stopped me from being the one who opened her mouth and saved someone else from a bad situation.

At the time when my student was being reduced to a body in a classroom of our department, I was trying to cope with being the object of what I would probably now call harassment. Back then it was seen rather as having "problems with colleagues." And of course there were people who were convinced (and still are) that I was as much of a problem as the others. It's in the past now

© ELIN LÅBY, 2022

and I have no wish or need to revisit that shame of not being able to fit in or even properly defend myself, but I remember an amazing person in the department of human resources—one of the few people who seemed to take my problems seriously. After having listened to some of my stories, she said without hesitation: "These are master suppression techniques, you need to learn how to deal with them." She explained to me how people would use these techniques in order to keep their own power and repress that of others. They were often directed against women and minorities, including younger colleagues or people considered "too young for the job." They could consist of things like making others feel invisible by ignoring their comments in a seminar or taking a phone call in the middle of a conversation, ridiculing or shaming them for their ideas or looks, or simply withholding information by not telling them about a meeting or event.

It was such an eye-opener. Suddenly I could see the pattern of what had been happening since I was a student, not just to me but all around me. All those seminars of listening to male colleagues repeating what female colleagues had just said, but suddenly receiving attention and praise. All the eye-rolling at things other people said or the way they dressed. All the times my colleagues had held back information, interrupted me or told me what to do, since they had "so much more experience." But recognizing and knowing didn't make it much easier to deal with. It was still shameful to be the object of other people's techniques! Why me? Why now? After all, I had worked in other places where I had been getting along just fine with people, being respected and pretty well liked. What did I do wrong?

It was also painful to come to understand that women use the same techniques as men, especially to other women. So far in my career, I hadn't had much of a problem with other women, but now that I had a proper job, all female colleagues, or at least those who were older than me, seemed to hate me. One told me how sad and worried she felt about the male candidate who didn't get the job. Others simply ignored my greetings in the corridor. Yet another invited me to lunch just to explain why I should never have been offered the position in the first place. It was devastating but slightly fascinating: to go through all that trouble just to humiliate someone over lunch! Oh, if I had only had that panic button ... But I didn't, and being humiliated by other women was somehow worse than being ignored or bullied by men. It felt like being back in high school, being watched by the mean girls who deliberately talk loud enough for you to hear. The feeling of wanting to disappear, just not get out of bed in the morning because you know there will be another day of whispering and smirks and dismissive comments.

I know that my memories are exaggerated. I know that I have made all this much worse than it was in my head, simply because it made me so miserable at the time. I'm convinced that some of the people around me never noticed. I kept my head high, I clearly stated my ideas and stood my ground. To some extent, I think that made it worse, provoking those who wanted me to show more respect not only for them as persons, but for the system as a whole. A decisive turning point for me was a discussion with a senior administrator, a man who had worked at the university for some thirty years and who had seen everything. We were having lunch and I complained, as usual, about how people treated me as a little girl and didn't see me as a real professor of X because I didn't fit the template, just couldn't live up to people's expectations. It wasn't the first time he heard me saying that. He looked at me and sighed, then said: "But look, now *you* are the professor of X at this university, so a professor of X at this university is just like you."

It sounds silly now that I try to put it on paper, but that was more useful than anything others had said to cheer me up or support me. It finally gave me the strength to fully accept my new role and not to care so much about what others think. It helped me decide who I wanted to be in academia, which was exactly whom I had already been but with more self-assurance and confidence. It didn't stop people from being mean to me, but it helped me cope.

And I don't regret my experience of harassment, regardless of how painful it was, because it has helped me to see and notice what happens around me. There are no panic buttons, so we all need to take our responsibility and raise our voice when colleagues misbehave. Those of us with permanent positions have the greatest responsibility because we have nothing to fear, but we are all part of the system, from undergraduate students to the vice chancellor: we *are* the system, so when the system fails, we need to do more than just blame it as an abstract entity. We speak up not only for ourselves, but for those who come after. To make the system better. I strongly believe in that, but some things in particular still worry me.

One is all the things I know I don't see, even though I think I'm being watchful. The anecdote of my student is only one example, but a scary one because it happened so close to me and I feel I should have known. Other things have happened in close proximity without any suspicions on my part. The male colleague whom I thought was simply a bad and lazy supervisor, even a bit of a womanizer, but who turned out to secretly harass his most attractive male students. How on earth could I not have known, having spent so much time at the center of that environment? Did I not want to see? Did I care less for the young men than I would have for young women? Was I less suspicious because of my gendered presumptions of who harasses whom? Why didn't anyone tell me? Did I not appear as a person who could be trusted? These questions are haunting me and I think they should. Only by questioning ourselves can we make things better.

The other is the way in which I see women behave to other women. I now most often get a better treatment than I did fifteen years ago, but that's clearly because of my current status and my age—I finally look old enough to be who I am, more or less. But the fact that I am treated better doesn't help when I see constant gender and age discrimination all around me, not only from men but from women. In fact, anything that stands out as odd is being commented on and often made fun of, regardless of what kind of deviation from the norm it is. Being a heterosexual man in gender studies is also a deviation of sorts, let's not forget about that. Or a straight blond woman in queer studies. We're all judgmental, that's for sure. And why should women be better than men, you might say—but why on earth should women keep suppressing other women when so many men are finally starting to change? The topic is very tricky, because criticizing other women is not *comme il faut*. It easily falls back on you: aren't you then a nasty woman who doesn't like other women? The commonplace of women being mean and competitive by nature is so prevalent, it even contributes to the way in which we accept all kind of things going on around us, because we don't want to be accused of being a bitch. It saddens me and drives me crazy.

This fear of being a trouble-maker or annoying in any way stops us all, but especially women, from acting as panic buttons, and in the end it really stands in the way of a better academic work environment. One of the things I learned from my advisor in the human resources department was how to confront people using master suppression techniques by simply asking then, nicely, what they meant by saying this or that. This is not something that always works, especially if the technique in question is to ignore someone. But this is where we need each other: if someone ignores me, I want to have a person there who says, "But why are you ignoring her?" When one of the men repeats something a woman just said but now gets acclaim, I want someone—and not always me—to say, "But that is exactly what X just said." When someone said, "Is green nail polish really suitable for a professor?" I wish someone had said, "Why do you comment on her looks?" We have to be each others' panic buttons—there is no other way. But if we all dare to do it, the behavior will change.

To my former student, I want to say that I'm sorry. I wish one of the other students had interrupted the teacher and said, "Why do you talk to her like that?" I wish I had been there for you, to tell you that you are not just a body, but that being a body is also not a bad thing. Perhaps I was too caught up in my own problems to see or understand yours, which is not an excuse but possibly an explanation. Yet I hope, and know, that you have learned from that experience, that you would never to treat others like that and that you would speak up if someone does it to someone else.

Wouldn't it be great to have panic buttons in every academic setting! But in the meantime, let's simply speak up. Nice could be the new brilliant.

CHAPTER 22

Quit

Thomas Oles

I called to him, rapidly stating what it was I wanted him to do—
namely, to examine a small paper with me. Imagine my surprise, nay,
my consternation, when, without moving from his privacy, Bartleby,
in a singularly mild, firm voice, replied, "I would prefer not to."

I sat awhile in perfect silence, rallying my stunned faculties.
Immediately it occurred to me that my ears had deceived me, or
Bartleby had entirely misunderstood my meaning. I repeated my
request in the clearest tone I could assume; but in quite as clear a
one came the previous reply, "I would prefer not to."

H. MELVILLE (*Bartleby the Scrivener: A Story of Wall Street*, 1997, p. 21)

∵

An early evening in late March, several weeks past my forty-eighth birthday.
I am seated in the departure lounge of Salt Lake City Airport, wrapped in a
Loden coat and staring into a half-empty plastic sushi tray on my lap.

I am on my way home from an academic conference. I chaired a panel on
fieldwork with some close colleagues. It all went well. Interest was expressed,
much future collaboration promised. It fell to me to sum up. *Fieldwork is about
chance*, I whispered, my voice ravaged by laryngitis, about risk. It is about the
learning that comes of being vulnerable, exposed, raw. In the field you can and
do get hurt. In the field you are never really in control, never really the master
of your fate, and in this it is like life, I said.

We call ourselves a tribe, this group. Who knows how we found each other.
We came together this year as we do most years, to affirm friendship, offer
support, steel ourselves anew for another year filled with the mundane disap-
pointments and degradations of university jobs. "Academic positions" is too
grandiose for us. We are not superstars. We do not write our own tickets. The
offices where we toil are small, they look onto loading docks and brick walls.
We live all over the world in places we tolerate, barely, for the paycheck. We

© THOMAS OLES, 2022 | DOI:10.1163/9789004521025_022

dream about someplace better. We spend (or spent, before the Covid year) a great deal of time in airplanes and even more in airports, waiting for flights delayed, rerouted, rebooked, cancelled. We have learned to turn those hours to our advantage. In departure lounges and airport bars, at ticket counters and security checkpoints and border control, we are always throwing together our next lecture, trudging through our students' prose thickets, tending the ever-unruly email gardens.

I had such high hopes for this hour. But the room is packed: every seat occupied, children splayed at their parents' feet, young people propped against the walls. To a one, all are device-entranced. Blue fluorescent light reaches every corner of the room and leaves only the darkening world beyond the plate glass as refuge. I lift my eyes, slowly trace the pink ridge of the Wasatch Front. It has just snowed.

You must quit, I think.

Do I say the words aloud? Do I even "think" them at all? They seem at once more and less than a thought. A conviction, an epiphany? No. This is a statement more like "it is Tuesday," banal and self-evident. No chain of reasoning leads up to it. It needs no argument, no explanation. It arrives just so, without fanfare, from some place far beyond thought, beyond reason or plan or consequence. But it demands utterance.

Now, years later, I know where the words come from. It is the "swamp brain," the reptile inside me fed up with the frontal lobe and its chatter, its endless *ifs* and *howevers* and *at the same times*. Fed up—and not fed.

You must eat, the reptile orders.

It has my attention now. It is angry. Yes. I suddenly realize I am dizzy, have not taken a single piece of food all day. I look back down at the pieces of sushi, each a sad little expression of the industrial food machine. I am about to take one when the frontal lobe barges back in, yelling.

crazy!
not so bad—
the children—
what about money?!
she will never accept—
things will surely—

I wait for the words to assemble themselves into sentences, sentences into arguments as they usually do. But the words are sheepish. They sit there, random once shiny objects sticking out of the muck. The ruler of the muck is amused. *Have your fun*, he says to the front brain. *Go ahead with your crystal palaces. They will all sink in the end.*

The reptile is in no hurry. It settles back while the words drag themselves to attention (they have had so much practice). *This institution is toxic*, they recite. *It will never change. They fired you without cause, then tried to cover it up. You hate your colleagues, you hate your students. They are poisoning you. And— final insult!—the pay is lousy, you are going broke.* And then suddenly emerges the sentence I will not forget, the sentence I will bear with me every day from then on, fully-formed, lapidary, like fully grown Athena from the head of Zeus: *I would rather never work in academia again than work in this university another minute.*

As rhetoric, not too bad. Perhaps the words will convince my skeptics. But the problem with words is that they are fickle. Once they get going there is no stopping them. Almost immediately, they turn on me:

> OK, *but what will you do? This work is all you know, all you can do. Sure universities have their problems. This one might be a bit worse than others, but how can you be certain you will end up—deserve to end up—with something better? Don't be so hasty. You are in no mental state to make such a consequential decision. Cool down, tot up the ledger. Wait a month or a year or two or three.*

My spirits sink with each clause, each premise. I am so damn good at this. But I am not the only one paying attention. The reptile is there, too, watching and waiting. It, too, knows a thing or two about words, and it has plans for me. I am just about to add the next proposition when it lunges forward, hisses and strikes:

Dear Dr Oles,

I understand that you received a UK Visas and Immigration letter stating that your residence card application has been refused. This letter confirms that you no longer have the right to work in the UK, therefore the University cannot legally continue your employment at this time. Your employment will terminate, as of today, on the grounds of statutory enactment. As this is a summary dismissal no notice or payment in lieu of notice is due to you. This decision has been reached after seeking

legal advice and guidance from the University's contact within the UKVI
Premium Customer Service Team who confirmed that the University can
no longer legally employ you.

Yours sincerely,
L R
Senior Human Resources Administrator

I step back and wait for the old sting. I know it well, for I have worried these
lines to threads since first reading them. They came attached to a late email
from my chair (last task, no doubt, before he headed off for the long weekend).
The email was festooned with empathy. I stood at my desk and stared at the
screen, words oozing and ramifying before me. My son was eight months old,
my daughter three years, mine the only salary. The world was inverted. There
was nowhere to turn, no succor to be found. I—we—were in hostile territory.
    I walked down to them in the park below, where they were playing with neigh-
bors. The smiles of pity, the polite assurances (all a mistake, will be put right soon
enough) enraged me. *They—will—regret—this!* I said, but thought: *You.*

Dear L R,

I was surprised and disappointed to receive your correspondence dated
06 April 2015, in which you inform me that I have been fired as of today
on grounds of "statutory enactment."
    I would have appreciated the opportunity to discuss my plans for
appealing this erroneous decision with you before being summarily
dismissed over the Easter holiday on the basis of advice from the "UKVI
Premium Customer Service Team." I have attached to this letter my Home
Office appeal and supporting evidence. I have also instructed my solic-
itor to review the circumstances of my dismissal, and request that you
immediately forward him complete transcripts of any and all legal advice
obtained from the Home Office in relation to my case.
    Naturally I have suspended execution of all duties associated with my
position pending resolution of this matter.

Sincerely,
&c

I wait for the venom to hit the skin. And wait. Adrenaline and dopamine ebb
away by increments. Still nothing. Finally, I relax. Not only have the words lost
their potency, I realize, they actually bore me. How can that be? Have I grown

immune from exposure? Am I just too weary, too worn down by airports and greasy food and stale conference hotel air? The reptile knows my brain too well to give me time to answer. As quickly as it deploys its venom it sucks it all back in again, like a film in reverse. All the words are gone. All, that is, except one.

Quit, a verb and a noun and an adjective. The 27-page entry in the OED tells me the word comes from Anglo-Norman and Old French *quiter*, meaning release, discharge or exonerate. To abandon, relinquish, renounce (an obligation or a debt). To leave, go away. To pay a penalty, to match or balance or redress. To rid of something undesirable or troublesome. Like retching.

Before the retching, though, the swoon. That sour certainty of sweat and bile. I mechanically avert my eyes from the sushi, try to ignore the food-court fragrance behind me. I look back out the window, where it has grown dark. I take imaginary gulps of jet fuel-spiked air. Perhaps I can get some work done. I reach down to the floor to pull out my laptop, then freeze. No. The reptile is not done with me, not yet. It crouches there, grinning, waiting. It knows.

The old definitions are ambiguous. *To rid of something troublesome*. But who is troublesome and who is troubled? Who is ridded and who does the ridding? What is matched, to whom is the penalty paid? Who owes, and who forgives? "I wolde wel quyte your hyre" Chaucer wrote, but Melville's Bartleby never says the word. His boss does.

Who is troublesome? I am troublesome.

I am a bad colleague.

I am not a "team player."

A team player would not file a grievance and insist on a formal apology— not when he is reinstated three weeks later and receives hush money in the bargain. A team player would not go to the press. He would not speak to a lawyer. He would keep his head and play the long game. He would go meekly before that tribunal of students convened by his "line manager" (we all work on the shop floor now), charged with ... what, exactly? Defying the learning outcomes? Going off-script on assessment? Holding a class meeting at an open-air museum? (Yes, I was indeed censured for this.)

No matter. Team players "welcome the opportunity to clear the air." Team players play ball. They do not tape record every meeting with superiors. Denied promotion to a rank they have already held in another institution, they do not protest. They accept the committee's verdict ("it was decided that you are not quite ready for promotion at this stage ...") with grace. They stick it out, try again next year and all the years after that.

Team players do not prefer not to.
Team players do not fold.
Team players do not quit.

It is not that I do not know the rules of this game. I know I should smile like a good colleague. But I have grown sullen in my privacy. I sit there, immobile. Some words are issuing from the Head of School seated beside me. *Student. Experience. Transparency. Openness. Mutual. Respect.* I turn and notice the straight teeth, the sequined shoes, the open palms, practiced and unquitterly. I remain a study in not smiling. When the floor is mine ("Thomas, is there anything you would like to add at this point?"), I turn and fix an icy gaze on my accusers. *Who called for this meeting?* I bark, deliberately rude. Much general squirming, then two hands slowly rise of the fifty assembled. Do I imagine the awkward laughter? It makes no difference. My sentence arrived on the docket.

Max Weber, now he knew the rules of this game as well as anyone. He saw them being written. In 1917 Weber gave a short speech to a group of doctoral students. To my mind it is the truest thing ever said and written on the modern university.

"What is the situation of a graduate student who is intent on an academic career?" he asked (Weber, 2004, p. 4). The first part of the answer concerns the transformation of the university into a capitalist bureaucracy, scholars into wage laborers alienated from the means of production. Their position is "as precarious as that of every other 'quasi-proletarian' in existence" (p. 4). But while "the old constitution of the university has become a fiction," Weber thought, one "feature peculiar to a university career" remained (p. 4). *Luck.*

> I personally owe it to a number of purely chance factors that I was appointed to a full professorship while still very young in a discipline in which people of my own age had undoubtedly achieved more [...] I have developed a keen eye for the undeserved fate of the many whom chance has treated, and continues to treat, in the opposite way and who have failed, for all their abilities, to obtain a position that should rightfully be theirs (Weber, 2004, p. 4)

Weber's luck ran out a year later. In 1918 he was dead of Spanish flu at the age of 53, my age today.

I see now what Weber saw then. But when, exactly, did I see it? *When* did I learn that I might be tolerated, but would never advance? *When* did I know not only not to smile, but that I would not forgive myself if I did? *When* did I learn to tape my conversations with superiors? *When* did I understand that each email, however trivial, was a piece of evidence in a case not yet assembled against me? When did I learn that I was a means to others' ends? *When*, come to think of it, did I even read that Weber essay in the first place? Was it the cause of my knowledge, or its effect?

I search for some watershed between the two selves, ante-quit and post-quit, AQ and PQ. The PQ self sits here now, years later, worrying these words. *That* self knows. But how exactly did the other self meet its end?

No matter. We make stories to forget, not remember. This one will do.

• •
•

I rise and walk over to the recycling station. I balance the empty tray (somehow I have eaten the remaining pieces) atop a hillock of identical landfill-bound receptacles, then start down the hallway back toward security. Eyes fixed on the psychedelic purple carpet, I walk slowly, gingerly, testing each creaky floor-board so as not to rouse the baby next door. That baby is a light sleeper. Worse, he babbles. Once he gets going there is no putting him down.

The reptile—now he does not like children. He is old and cranky. He wants his peace and quiet, and he wants my undivided attention. Will he follow me a little way? Am I worth his time?

So far so good. I continue down the concourse, lazily contemplating the variegated doughnuts and Brigham Young effigies. I wait for the front brain to awake, the old fighting words to return. But the baby sleeps on. And then I realize it is no accident. The reptile has done more than follow. It is there on my back, black claws digging into my shoulders, long head pivoting slowly back and forth. I feel the stored heat through my coat. It has me now. I stop amid the current of travelers, look without seeing. My muscles go slack, my frame goes heavy and—I float. *Thanatosis* they call this, tonic immobility. So that's it. I am playing dead, and the dead are done with words.

I let myself be swept down the hallway tributaries of Salt Lake City International Airport, emerging just enough, at each successive terminus, to swim back up again. An hour, maybe two has passed when I hear the muffled syllables of my name. *Last call ... Proceed immediately ... Your baggage will be off-loaded ...* I crawl onto the bank, stand up and enter a newspaper stand. *Do not exceed two capsules daily*, the maximum strength sedative label admonishes. I rip open the box, take six and bear my precious passenger toward the gate.

• •
•

Later, but not much later, you will run out of the house, down the steps and into the spring night. You will not have a map. Before long you will remember your empty pockets and bad shoes. Not too late to turn around, but you will continue, each step another sunk cost. One mile, two miles past grey houses and gravid rhododendrons. Three miles and you will feel the land slope on your breath. You will see the mountains, giant black waves frozen mid-crest, and press on, upward, the way choosing you. At no place in particular you will stop, turn, look. The city is a distant yellow galaxy at your feet. You stand there in the rain and blackness, waiting.

So this will be your life now. You will work for universities again, but never again will you be not quit. That fall, you will understand, is absolute. The road back (you will know because you will try to find it) is washed out, gone. A knowing means (you will know because you will try to do it) cannot bend itself back into an unknowing end.

Well, what on earth kind of life will that be, you ask. A life exposed and raw, certainly. A life more resigned and remote, probably. Some will say, a life poisoned by cynicism and darkness. But also, you will come to learn, a life less fearful. A life more fierce, more truly your own. A life—here now is another, much bigger word—more free.

The moment of change is nothing special. You will not see it coming. One day, like Bartleby, like me, you will simply withdraw behind the screen, to your privacy, and remain there. The event is not heroic or grandiose. You cannot give it a name. It is just what happens when the reptile, long mute, finally demands to speak. It is just what happens when you see—in some airport, stuck in traffic, almost too late—you are a means, not an end. It is just what happens when you cut your losses and walk away from the table. It is what happens, what will happen, when you quit.

References

Melville, H. (1997). *Bartleby the scrivener: A story of Wall Street*. Simon & Schuster.
Weber, M. (2004). Science as a vocation. In M. Weber, *The vocation lectures* (D. Owen & T. B. Strong, Eds.; R. Livingstone, Trans.). Hackett. (Original work published 1917)

CHAPTER 23

Diving Deeper

The Redemptive Power of Metaphor

Helen Sword

When the higher education research and development center that I had nur-
tured and led for seven years was quietly taken behind the barn and shot in the
head (figuratively speaking), I felt disempowered, grief-stricken and angry. The
whole operation was performed in such a secretive, cynical way—apparently
designed by senior management to avert criticism rather than to ensure insti-
tution-wide consultation—that whatever faith I had once held in my university's self-declared values of inclusiveness, fairness and research-led inquiry
was left battered and broken at the scene of the crime, along with some of
my center's most cherished initiatives, not to mention the careers of several
valued colleagues.

Unable to avert this abuse of institutional power (although goodness knows
I tried!), I decided to focus on changing what I could control: my own emotional response to the event. Harnessing the power of language to shape reality, I turned to metaphor to help me restore and restory my personal narrative.
I started by interrogating the shot-behind-the-barn metaphor that I had been
using to frame that narrative, posing a series of questions adapted from a
rubric that I had developed as part of an earlier research project on the emotional habits of academic writers from across the disciplines:[1]

1. *Domain* Does my metaphor invoke the natural world, the world of human
   experience, or both?
   Key principle: DEEPER metaphors typically invoke both nature and
   culture.

2. *Emphasis* Does my metaphor emphasize the event itself, the unfolding of
   the event, or both?
   Key principle: DEEPER metaphors typically encompass both process and
   product.

3. *Emotion* Does my metaphor convey positive emotions about the event,
   negative emotions, or both?

Key principle: DEEPER metaphors typically emphasize the positive aspects of an event while also acknowledging its negative side.

4. *People* Am I present in my metaphor? Are other people part of my story?
Key principle: DEEPER metaphors typically include both the subject and the subject's social networks in the narrative.

5. *Empowerment* Am I an active, engaged protagonist who faces challenges and is open to learning new skills, or does the metaphor depict me a powerless pawn caught up in someone else's game? (Do I control the story, or does the story control me?)
Key principle: DEEPER metaphors typically grant personal agency to the subject while also acknowledging the influence of powers beyond their control.

6. *Resonance* Does the metaphor have personal resonance—that is, does it speak to me in some meaningful way? Does it have universal resonance—that is, does it speak to others?
Key principle: DEEPER metaphors are personally relevant to the subject while also speaking to a wider audience.

These questions are intended not as "either/or" alternatives but as "both/and" prompts leading to the development of what I call "DEEPER metaphors." The "taken behind the barn and shot" metaphor, I quickly realized, fails the DEEPER test on almost every count. For example, it focuses on a fait accompli rather than a process of becoming; it presents a narrative of helplessness in which my colleagues and I feature as a passive victims rather than as human beings possessed of agency, spirit and heart; and it allows no space for positive transformation or intellectual growth.

DEEPER metaphors are capacious and complex, embracing not only the positive aspects of human existence but also what educator Parker J. Palmer (2007) calls the "shadow side," the sharp edge that leads us to change and grow. Diving DEEPER into the emotional wreckage of my own experience—a seabed strewn with sadness and shame—I eventually rose to the surface with a new metaphor, recasting my shot-behind-the-barn narrative as an intrepid ocean voyage instead:

The seagoing waka

Seven years before the big wave hit, twenty intrepid voyagers set sail in a seagoing *waka*, a large double-hulled canoe designed to traverse vast distances and explore unknown territories. As their navigator and *rangatira* (leader), it was my job to set the course, read the star signs and inspire my loyal crew to pull the oars, trim the sails and keep us on an even keel. Together we rode the ocean currents and caught the tradewinds; together we sailed past whirlpools and through tempests; from time to time we forged alliances with other adventurers, lashing our vessel to theirs to share stories and trade provisions. When at last our beloved waka went down, swamped by a tsumani too massive for us to weather, the bonds that we had forged during our seven-year adventure helped us all make it safely to shore, the weakest among us buoyed up by the strongest. Some of my shipmates went off to crew on other boats; some built new lives working the land; a few ended up marooned on the rocks, too exhausted and dispirited to pick up the pieces of their shattered careers and start anew. As for me, I climbed to the top of a hill and built a lighthouse there, a beacon of hope for weary travelers in need of a safe harbor as they traverse those same perilous seas.

My new metaphor helped me to shift the focus of my story from institutional violence to human agency and to paint an emotional landscape tinged with darkness yet suffused by light. However, when I subjected the metaphor to the twelve questions from the DEEPER rubric, I uncovered two central weaknesses. Firstly, my ocean voyage metaphor lacks personal relevance or resonance; I have never even sailed on, much less captained, a seagoing waka and have no direct affiliation with the Polynesian cultures (Māori, Tongan and Samoan) from which I have appropriated some of the metaphor's most compelling features: the seagoing waka; the lashing of the canoes, the art of star navigation. Secondly, in my eagerness to reclaim agency and empowerment for myself and my crew, I have allowed the metaphor to go overboard (so to speak) in its representation of administrative decision-makers as an unstoppable force of nature. We were not in fact struck down by a natural disaster such as a tidal wave or a tempest; rather, our vessel was deliberately sabotaged by senior managers in an act that resembled the sinking of the Rainbow Warrior (the Greenpeace ship infamously limpet-bombed by French government agents in New Zealand to prevent its crew from protesting nuclear testing in the South Pacific), rather than that of, say, the Edmund Fitzgerald (the Lake Superior freighter that sank with all hands aboard after reportedly being swamped by a rogue wave).

While neither of these shortcomings would, on its own, necessarily have forced me to scupper my waka metaphor, together they contributed to a nagging feeling that the sea voyage trope wasn't quite working. Reluctantly I abandoned ship and cast about for a redemptive metaphor with greater personal resonance and a darker edge. Eventually I settled on the art of mosaic-making, a metaphor that I have frequently used to describe my writing practice and now broadened to include academic leadership as well:

The mosaic path

I love collecting objects that have been discarded or passed over by others—stained glass offcuts, chipped crockery, river stones, seashells—and assembling them into new works of art, creating unexpected juxtapositions of color and form. When the intricate mosaic walkway that I had spent seven years designing and grouting into place was bulldozed by autocratic university administrators and replaced with a straight and narrow footpath, I understood their motivation: my joyfully meandering pathway was too non-conformist, its colors too rich, its energy too vibrant, to suit their dehumanizing neoliberal agenda. But a mosaic, having been created from fragments, can be reassembled in new configurations even after having been blown apart. I now spend my days on a beautiful South Pacific island laying out another crazy paving, this one even more colorful and playful than the last. This time, however, the pathway runs through my own property rather than the university's; never again will I risk having my life and art consigned to a dumpster by philistine landlords.

The mosaic metaphor helped me recognize my former academic leadership role—indeed, my entire scholarly career—as a creative practice that, like all art-making, is richly fulfilling but fraught with risk. At the same time, the DEEPER rubric prompted me to pose some hard questions thrown up by the metaphor: for example, what does it mean to be a scholar whose creative energies feed on the smashing of icons? As a leader, do I treat those I lead as mere tesserae in my mosaic, to be manipulated and glued into place? My metaphor becomes even more powerful and emotionally nuanced when I cast light into those shadows, reaffirming my commitment to what academic activist Kathleen Fitzpatrick (2019) calls "generous thinking" and celebrating my colleagues' roles as co-creators of a pathway that we designed and built together. Like me, they are now picking up the scattered pieces and laying out new mosaics of their own. In the years to come, I expect that our paths will intersect in unanticipated ways, linked by a shared history and ethos.

I do not mean to suggest here that metaphorical language can always pave over pain, nor that beleaguered academics should respond to all administrative abuses of power as I have done in this instance, by retreating to an island (literally as well figuratively) and giving up on institutional activism. My decision to start my own business as an international writing consultant, building new pathways into writing for scholars around the world, has come towards the end of a long career spent fighting in the university trenches for causes such as gender equity, cultural inclusiveness and student-centered teaching. If I were ten years younger, a different set of metaphors might have inspired me to gird my loins emotionally and return to the fray. (Rest assured, however, that I would not have persisted with the military trope for long; its shadow side is too dark to dwell in, even if academic life does sometimes feel like a war zone.) Either way, redemptive metaphors have helped me find my way forward. Indeed, the very process of writing this essay has accelerated my transformation from a self-perceived victim of circumstance to a maker and shaper who has taken my future into my own hands. By diving DEEPER into metaphor, I have salvaged my sense of personal agency, affirmed my creative resilience and emerged from a fetid swamp of negative emotions into clearer air.

Note

1   Adapted from an exercise in Sword (2019).

References

Fitzpatrick, K. (2019). *Generous thinking: A radical approach to saving the university.* Johns Hopkins University Press.

Palmer, P. J. (2007). *The courage to teach: Exploring the inner landscape of a teacher's life* (10th anniversary ed.). Jossey-Bass.

Sword, H. (2019). Snowflakes, splinters and cobblestones: Metaphors for writing. In S. Farquhar & E. Fitzpatrick (Eds.), *Narrative and metaphor: Innovative methodologies and practice* (pp. 39–55). Springer.

The Privilege of Writing One's Story and Reading Those of Others

Ingela Nilsson

It is 2021 and we are preparing this volume for submission and peer review.

In a museum shop I see a notebook, on the cover it says: "If you don't write your story, who will?" I like this, I buy a whole bunch and hand them out to my friends.

I read a new book by Elif Shafak, *How to Stay Sane in an Age of Division* (2020). She argues that if you cannot tell your own story, you will not be willing to listen to the stories of others. This suits both my personal view and my academic interests, so I talk a lot about this book, plan for an essay or a blog post about the transformative power of stories to bring people together.

I take part in a seminar on minority narratives and my colleague, a historian specializing in the Armenian minority of Turkey, points out that stories—despite their potential for consolidation and understanding, also risk creating or sustaining conflicts and make violence on the one whose story is not heard or understood. This statement is unsettling in its simplicity. I repeat to myself what has by now become almost a mantra: if I don't tell my story, then someone else may. But is it really that easy?

Critical storytelling has received increasing attention in recent years and even formed a new field of studies—with this series as an important platform for publication. In the wake of classical and postclassical narratology, storytelling has come to play a significant role in several academic fields, not the least in Psychology and Conflict Studies. A basic assumption for most of these studies is that narration is a human constant, or that "the act of constructing stories is a natural human process" (Pennebaker & Seagal, 1999, p. 1243). In that sense, the position of Roland Barthes, one of the foundational fathers of narratology, is still formative for the field: narrative is seen as "international, transhistorical, transcultural: it is simply there, like life itself" (Barthes, 1977, p. 79).[1] A central implication, then, is that to understand how stories function is a way to understand human beings. For someone like me, a literary historian who has been working on narratological angles of both fictional and factual texts for some twenty years, this is obviously a crucial assumption.

At the same time, the increasingly common cue to "control your narrative"—a kind of self-help exhortation to "craft the life you want for yourself" (Riley, 2017)—gives the impression that each individual story is "true," as long as it is personal and sincerely narrated as a kind of "serious storytelling" (Lugmayr et al., 2016). But it goes without saying that if each individual has their own story and their own version of any given event, these stories are bound to clash with each other. This is indeed what is happening at this point in time, on both micro and macro levels of society: from the presentation of "my story" on individual Instagram accounts to recurring major narratives of Male and Female, East and West, Christianity and Islam. In such a situation, is the encouragement to craft and tell our own story even helpful?

The contributions in this volume are responses to such an encouragement: please share your story of academia with us, of harassment, abuse, of unfair treatment, so that we may feel less alone in our daily struggle. Share not only your anger and disappointment, but also your experience and strategies— help us find ways to make things better. And do that in any form you want, as long as it is candid. Unless you have skipped the previous chapters and went straight for the epilogues, you have just read the results of this request. It is a collection of tales and experiences as diverse as the individuals behind them, yet sadly consistent.

If classical narratology focuses primarily on structure and order, storytelling is rather about the social, cultural and political activity of telling and sharing stories. It takes us back to where Barthes started: as human beings we need stories not only for entertainment and comfort, but also for our shared memories, for stating moral values, for education and cultural preservation. Critical storytelling takes us one step further in the direction of the individual: its aim is to find alternative perspectives, to question previously unquestioned narratives and norms, to expose oppression and envision possibilities for change.[2] In that sense, it wishes to avoid metanarratives and reach for minority angles. Such a definition makes me think of Svetlana Alexievich as a critical storyteller par excellence, relentlessly telling the stories of the unheard. The fact that she was awarded the 2015 Nobel Prize shows how not only important but also appreciated such perspectives are: "for her polyphonic writings, a monument to suffering and courage in our time."[3]

Ironically, Alexievich was nominated by a committee consisting of Swedish Academy members tacitly accepting the kind of gender-based abusive practices that would cause an international scandal a couple of years later; this is a good example of how hypocrisy is present on all levels of society, including its most sacred intellectual circles.[4] But regardless of those events, the polyphony underlined in the press release of the Academy is essential, not only in Alexiev-ich's writings, but also in critical storytelling in general: individual voices may not easily be heard, but the function of polyphony is infinitely useful. First, it shows that the individual story is unique and not like any other; second, it demonstrates that all these individual stories have several similarities despite their differences; and third, it offers comfort and support to an endless num-ber of individuals thanks to the above. Polyphony, moreover, demands of the reader or listener a critical stance, since many voices offer no unanimous mes-sage. They demand critical reflection, which in turn encourages the investiga-tion of possibilities for change (Morley, 2014).

The stories collected here all bear witness to such theoretical processes, even if representations such as poems, drawings and fragments are presented with-out footnotes or academic references. As editors we have also had the privilege of following the benefits of the writing process itself—our own, of course, but also that of our contributors. Many of them have underlined the painful and yet liberating experience of "writing their story," and here the narratological perspective needs to be brought back in: this is not just a question of "being heard," but also about finding the right form and structure for your narrative. Because it is the construction of a sequence of events, argue psychologists, that helps us deal with emotional distress:

> Once an experience has structure and meaning, it would follow that the emotional effects of that experience are more manageable. Constructing stories facilitates a sense of resolution, which results in less rumination and eventually allows disturbing experiences to subside gradually from conscious thought. Painful events that are not structured into a narrative format may contribute to the continued experience of negative thoughts and feelings. (Pennebaker & Seagal, 1999, p. 1243)

So forming a story about life experiences improves mental health, something that has marked psychotherapy since Freud. This is related to the sense of meaning that a narrative sequence creates; in the words of Hannah Arendt, "the story reveals the meaning of what would otherwise remain an intolerable sequence of events" (Arendt, 1979, p. xx; Wilkinson, 2014). This is how myths and folktales play such a central role in most cultures, by offering models of interpretation for life experiences: stories offer good or bad examples of behav-ior and in this way helps socialization, from antiquity onwards (Ingemark & Asplund Ingemark, 2021, esp. p. 151). As society changes, or stories travel from one culture to another, the narratives inevitably change too, offering new mod-els of understanding life.

Storytelling thus remains at the very heart of who we are and how we understand ourselves, but a problem (among many) is that our own story can only be seen and constructed in hindsight. As noted by feminist philosopher Adriana Cavarero, "Life cannot be lived like a story, because the story always comes afterwards, it results; it is unforeseeable and uncontrollable, just like life." (Cavarero, 2000, p. 3). This reveals the problem with the notion of "control your life-story" projected in social media and by self-help guides, noted above, because it means that one tries to impose order where there is none (yet). Indeed, another kind of story that is common in our time—conspiracy narratives—function in a very similar way: they transform senseless events or "facts" into more or less well-ordered accounts (Butter, 2021). Somehow we need to find a way to deal with the constant friction between our own story—the construction and telling of which can lead to our well-being—and the overarching narratives of a global world, in which many of us feel lost and alienated.

Critical storytelling is an important tool here, employed in many forms and for multiple purposes, from "the slippery slopes of silencing" of women (Solnit, 2014, pp. 4–8) and the #MeToo movement to the "common story" of minorities and refugees (e.g. Nguyen, 2018). And despite the perhaps overly critical comments above—which, I think, have to be part of Critical Storytelling—I do think that we have to follow Shafak's cue and start by telling our own story, in order to be willing to listen to those of others:

> If wanting to be heard is one side of the coin, the other side is being willing to listen. The two are inextricably connected. When convinced that no one—especially those in places of power and privilege—is really paying attention to our protests and demands we will be less inclined to listen to others, particularly to people whose views differ from ours. […] if perpetuated and made routine, the feeling of being systematically unheard will slowly, gradually, seal our ears, and then seal our hearts. (Shafak, 2020, p. 15)

This may seem like a simple and even naïve observation, but it takes us back to my colleague's caution about the violent potential of stories. Indeed, narratives not only benefit mutual understanding, they also "constitute crucial means *of generating, sustaining, mediating, and representing conflict* at all levels of social organization" (Briggs, 1996, p. 3; my emphasis). When Jean François Lyotard in his famous book *La condition postmoderne* (1979) described Postmodernism as "incredulity toward metanarratives" and urged a focus on local stories rather than grand narratives, he initiated a new way of thinking about competing stories as fractured narration. This was later applied in postcolonial theory to the way in which both imperial narrative and indigenous narratives are always part of the conflict: the stories that conflicting groups tell themselves and each other are, in practice, the ideological fuel of either strife or reconciliation. So if we believe in storytelling as a method in both academic and social contexts, we need to be willing to acknowledge also those qualities and potential abuses of narration, finding a critical balance between the singular/individual and the plural/collective in both representation and analysis.

In a recent and somewhat unexpected publication by Princeton University Press—a graphic novel on political violence in Turkey in the 1970s—social anthropologist Jenny White has chosen this particular media in order to reflect the kaleidoscopic or fractured nature of the stories she came across in her interviews:

> Why a graphic novel? When doing the interviews, I had no specific agenda and allowed myself to be surprised by people's stories and motivations. People's memories of the time were vivid and often they seemed to relive their experiences in the telling. It occurred to me that academic analysis flattened these stories as it folded them into discussions of abstract issues, like factionalism. Perhaps I could make the same points by allowing people to tell their stories in graphic form and thereby retain the nuances and contradictions of history as it is lived. (White & Gündüz, 2021, p. 9)

The result is a vivid and truly polyphonic narrative: personal and emotional, yet educational and critical.

White's emphasis on nuances and contradictions must be taken into account not only for history, but for human expression at large. Stories clearly possess more power than is often acknowledged and they should therefore be taken seriously, not just as a means of expressing one's own identity, emotions and aspirations, but also—or perhaps above all—as a way of understanding others in relation to ourselves. In a world currently disposed towards group-think and filter bubbles, we need to heed not only those who are systematically unheard, but also those who want to be heard for all the wrong reasons. If we do not accept the kaleidoscope that include accounts we do not like or agree with, we cannot expect tolerance and solidarity from others.

Critical storytelling must accordingly include self-examination and acceptance. When we narrate our experiences, as we have done in this volume, we should challenge both ourselves and our readers. This act of sharing stories should not be merely about feeling better for having presented our version of events, but also about accepting different perspectives even in shared experiences. We must be willing to listen also to those we see as perpetrators, provided that they would be willing to listen to us. There is no point in creating or sustaining conflicts through storytelling, only in using it for expanding our cognitive horizons and engaging in a process of mutual learning about each other and ourselves.

Let us be honest: academia has not exactly taken a lead in this respect, but it is never too late for change. It has already been thirty years since Thomas E. Barone urged his readers to employ the method of story sharing in educational contexts in order "to make palpable and comprehensible the pain and cruelty of isolation inflicted on people" (students, teachers and administrators). He wanted us to use our "privileges to tell stories that enable readers to locate the sources of that pain." That is what we—the voices in this volume—have now done: we have used our privilege to tell stories, now it is up to you, our readers, to read them with a critical gaze and then tell yours.

Acknowledgement

The writing of this chapter has been undertaken within the frame of the research program Retracing Connections (https://retracingconnections.org/), financed by Riksbankens Jubileumsfond (M19-0430:1).

Notes

1   The assumption of universalism has been rejected by postclassical feminist narratology, arguing that it was "founded on an androcentric bias" (Page, 2006, p. 4). Beyond that academic field, it seems that narrative as a human constant remains rather unchallenged, but see also below on narrative as inevitably polyphonic and fractured.
2   This is how the Critical Storytelling series is defined at https://brill.com/view/serial/CSTO and how it is defined in several prefaces to previous volumes, esp. Braniger and Jacoby (2019, pp. xv–xvi); for the confusing claim that they have coined the term, see however Barone (1992), also cited below.
3   For the press release in different languages, see https://www.nobelprize.org/prizes/literature/2015/press-release/
4   One of the best accounts of these events remains Voss Gustafsson (2019), translated into several languages but sadly enough not into English; see https://ahlanderagency.com/books/the-club-a-chronicle-of-power-and-abuse-at-the-heart-of-the-nobel-scandal/

References

Barone, T. E. (1992). Beyond theory and method: A case of critical storytelling. *Theory into Practice, 31*(2), 142–146.

Barthes, R. (1977). Introduction to the structural analysis of narrative. In *Image, music, text* (Essays selected and translated by S. Heath) (pp. 79–124). Fontana Press.

Braniger, C. J., & Jacoby, K. M. (Eds.). (2019). *Critical storytelling in millennial times: Undergraduates share their stories of struggle.* Brill.

Briggs, C. (Ed.). (1996). *Disorderly discourse: Narrative, conflict, and social inequality.* Oxford University Press.

Butter, M. (2021). Conspiracy theories—Conspiracy narratives. *DIEGESIS. Interdisciplinary E-Journal for Narrative Research/Interdisziplinäres E-Journal für Erzählforschung, 10*(1), 97–100. https://www.diegesis.uni-wuppertal.de/index.php/diegesis/article/download/415/601

Cavarero, A. (2000). *Relating narratives: Storytelling and selfhood.* (Translated and with an Introduction by P. A. Kottman). Routledge. (Original work published 1997).

Ingemark, D., & Asplund Ingemark, C. (2021). Socialization: Fairytales as vehicles of moral messages. In D. Felton (Ed.), *A cultural history of fairy tales in antiquity* (pp. 149–168). Bloomsbury Academic.

Lugmayr, A., et al. (2016). Serious storytelling—A first definition and review. *Multimedia Tools and Applications, 76*(14), 15707–15733.

Morley, C. (2014). Using critical reflection to research possibilities for change. *British Journal for Social Work, 44*(6), 1419–1435.

Nguyen, V. T. (Ed.). (2018). *The displaced: Refugee writers on refugee lives.* Abrams Press.

Page, R. E. (2006). *Literary and linguistic approaches to feminist narratology.* Palgrave Macmillan.

Pennebaker, J. W., & Seagal, J. D. (1999). Forming a story: The health benefits of narrative. *Journal of Clinical Psychology, 55*(10), 1243–1254.

Riley, M. (2017). *Control your narrative.* https://medium.com/the-ascent/control-your-narrative-d55602295dd7

Shafak, E. (2020). *How to stay sane in an age of division.* Profile Books.

Solnit, R. (2014). *Men explain things to me.* Haymarket Books.

Voss Gustafsson, M. (2019). *Klubben. En undersökning.* Albert Bonniers förlag.

White, J., & Gündüz, E. (2021). *Turkish kaleidoscope: Fractured lives in a time of violence.* Princeton University Press.

Wilkinson, L. R. (2004). Hannah Arendt on Isak Dinesen: Between storytelling and theory. *Comparative Literature, 56*(1), 77–98.

EPILOGUE

Gathering Voices for a Better Academic Workplace

Julie Hansen

> Academic life, then, is a wild venture.
> MAX WEBER ("Wissenschaft als Beruf," 1917/2008, p. 30)

∴

What conclusions can be drawn from the stories in this book? Are they just a handful of exceptional cases, or the tip of an iceberg? It is difficult to generalize about the academic workplace. The opening dictum in Leo Tolstoy's novel *Anna Karenina*—each unhappy family is unhappy in its own way—arguably holds true for university departments, too. Happy departments are characterized by transparency, constructive leadership and what organizational researchers call "psychological safety." Amy C. Edmondson (2019) defines psychological safety as

> a climate in which people are comfortable expressing and being themselves. [...] they feel comfortable sharing concerns and mistakes without fear of embarrassment or retribution. They are confident that they can speak up and won't be humiliated, ignored, or blamed. [...] They tend to trust and respect their colleagues. ("Introduction," e-book, n.p.)

By contrast, the symptoms of unhappy departments can be hard to diagnose and even harder to treat. If, as David Damrosch (1995) posits, "the modern university is built upon alienation and aggression" (p. 78), then those of us who inhabit it risk becoming blind to these qualities. After all, stereotypes of academia encourage us to tolerate divergent behavior. As Darla Twale and Barbara De Luca (2008) observe, "College faculty have been characterized as quirky, eccentric, and absent-minded. Unexpected behaviors are considered normal to the insider in addition to being thought simply odd to any outsider" (p. 101).[1] Reputation-conscious university administrations have been known to go to great lengths to cover up power abuse. Academics, for their part, are often poorly equipped to recognize it when it occurs.

Fortunately, academics seeking to better understand the psychosocial dynamics of their profession will now find a growing body of scholarship devoted to work environment issues in higher education. Other sectors were the focus of the earliest research on adult bullying that came out of Scandinavia in the 1990s, but since the turn of the millennium, behavioral scientists in Australia, Europe and North America have begun to focus more on academia.[2] A number of recent studies indicate that academic work environments are particularly susceptible to bullying, harassment and power abuse.[3] As Kenneth Westhues (2004) notes, "a university is a complex maze of overlapping rules, purposes, positions, committees, and codes," and thus the mechanisms of power abuse are also complex (p. VI). Twale and De Luca (2008) observe that the "unique organization structure of the university supports an equally unique academic culture," which in turn provides "a breeding ground for incivility, bullying, and mobbing" (p. 93). Loraleigh Keashly and Joel H. Neuman (2010) maintain that "the academic environment has a number of organizational and work features that increase the likelihood of hostile interpersonal behaviors" (p. 49).

As the stories in this book show, power abuse looks different from different positions in the academic hierarchy (see Chapter 10 by Hanna McGinnis, Ana C. Núñez and Anonymous 4 for a discussion of this point). Culture-specific dimensions can be discerned within this global problem, as the anonymous author of Chapter 17 shows. Power abuse can also play out differently in different educational, economic and political systems, with harsher instruments of abuse occurring in authoritarian regimes. Nevertheless, organizational psychologists and sociologists have identified a number of factors associated with power abuse in academia. These include (but are not limited to) low job security, institutional structures, organizational culture and a disconnect between academics' own ideals of their profession, on the one hand, and real working conditions, on the other.

1   Peculiarities of the Academic Workplace

Already in 1917, the German sociologist and political economist Max Weber devoted a lecture entitled "Wissenschaft als Beruf" to a consideration of factors that influence scholarly careers.[4] One of these is sheer luck. Whether an academic achieves promotion is, according to Weber, "a matter of pure *chance*." This observation is worth quoting at length:

> Of course, chance is not the only factor, but it is an unusually powerful factor. I can think of almost no other career on earth in which it has such a large part to play. I am especially well placed to say this, as I personally owe it to a few instances of sheer chance that at a very early age I was

appointed to a full professorship in a discipline in which at that time my contemporaries had undoubtedly achieved more than I had. And I feel that this experience has given me a keener awareness of the undeserved fate of those many others whom chance has treated unkindly and still does, and who despite all their ability failed to reach the position they merited as a result of this mechanism of selection. (Weber, 1917/2008, p. 28)

A century later, journalist Sarah Jaffe argues that in contemporary American academia, "the distinction between tenure track and adjunct track is an accident of timing" (2021, p. 163). Those lucky to be hired into a tenure-track position must cope with years of pressure to impress the senior colleagues who will ultimately decide whether tenure is granted (for more on this, see the chapters by Antony T. Smith and Ken Robertson). Those hired as adjuncts on part-time or short-term contracts comprise a growing "untenured underclass" lacking job security and decent working conditions (Fleming, 2021, p. 94; Jaffe, 2021, pp. 161–181).

This situation has been exacerbated by academia's adoption of neoliberal principles. New public management (examined in the chapters by Cecilia Mörner and Wim Verbaal) has been implemented differently in different places, but everywhere, academics report increased workloads and chronic stress, as well as subjection to what is termed "corrosive" or "destructive leadership" (Thornton, 2004; Einarsen et al., 2007).[5] Many point out a fundamental incompatibility of the mission of higher education with neoliberal tendencies, such as quantification, commodification and commercialization (Davies, 2005; Fleming, 2021). Francesca Coin (2017) observes that in the wake of neoliberalized academia, "scholars have felt a growing conflict between their ethical ideals and the array of measured, meaningless and bureaucratized tasks that fill their lives" (p. 707). Neoliberal audit culture and top-heavy management clash with established traditions of collegial self-governance in academia (Jaffe, 2021, pp. 161–181). "Fear is now the go-to technique for motivating faculty and staff," concludes Peter Fleming. "Managers choose this method since it's far easier to issue orders fait accompli via email than talk with colleagues and build a consensus" (Fleming, 2021, p. 4). Bronwyn Davies (2005) asks, "What then can we say that academic work is? Within neoliberal regimes we can no longer say it is the life of the intellect and of the imagination" (p. 1).[6] All this serves to create "conditions that incite incivility, workplace bullying, and other forms of employee abuse" (Zabrodska et al., 2011).

Jaffe discerns a downward trajectory in the conditions of academic work that is pushing more and more of the professoriate into the security-lacking precariat, depriving them at the same time of power and putting them at greater risk of exploitation.[7] Jaffe describes "precarious academics" (along with artists, musicians, writers and athletes) as "workers who are expected to find the work itself rewarding, as a place to express their own unique selves, their particular genius. In these jobs, we're likely to be told that we should be grateful to be able to work in the field at all, as there are hundreds of people who wish they had the opportunity to do jobs half as cool" (2021, p. 20).

Of course, work won't love you back, as noted in the apt title of Jaffe's recent book-length critique of this "labor-of-love ethic" (2021). The belief in a calling is a double-edged sword for academics, to whom it accords "a sense of purpose, meaning and satisfaction" (Barcan, 2018, p. 106), yet also renders them vulnerable to burnout and exploitation (Jaffe, 2021, pp. 161–181; Malesic, 2022).[8] Academic culture encourages self-exploitation "as a meritorious form of conduct" (Coin, 2017, p. 711), manifest on the individual level in feelings of inadequacy and failure, as well as the belief that the solution lies in working ever harder and longer.[9] In this way, academics are poorly served by their own devotion to their work. "The constant mis-match between organizational strain and personal values," notes Coin, "produce[s] burn-out and ethical conflicts particularly in those individuals who perceive academic labor as a passion or a labor of love" (2017, pp. 712–713). Many academics identify closely with their chosen profession, which means their sense of self can be on the line when things go wrong with the work environment. "Rather than a labor of love, academic labor sometimes appears an abusive relationship, an exploitative system characterized by high expectations and uncertain prospects" (Coin, 2017, p. 713). In this respect, the view of academics taken by the burgeoning field of Critical University Studies—i.e. an unembellished understanding of them as *workers* performing *labor*—provides a necessary corrective to the prevalent (and often self-destructive) devotionalist approach.

The above factors—job precarity, neoliberal transformations and academics' high ideals of their own profession (the list is not exhaustive)—all increase the risk of power abuse. They also contribute to a culture of fear, shame and silence, which indirectly support power abuse by serving to isolate and alienate academics from one another, making it easier for department chairs, deans and other administrators to divide and conquer faculty.[10] As Damrosch writes, "Alienation breeds a defensive aggressiveness; this aggression in turn magnifies the alienation, and the whole unhappy cycle begins again" (1995, p. 96). The question is how to break this cycle.

2   Where Do We Go from Here?

Although not all the stories in this book can be said to have happy endings, they illustrate various constructive responses to power abuse in academia. While some of the authors have chosen to leave academia, others remain within its walls (at least for the time being). It is a testament to the deep investment of academics' identity in their profession that a decision to quit is often met with surprise and even disbelief on the part of colleagues. This kind of investment can make it hard to imagine alternatives to the status quo, rendering "the idea of leaving voluntarily inconceivable" (Barcan, 2018, p. 115).

Yet more and more academics who feel their working conditions to be untenable are taking this leap—at least if we are to judge from the new genre dubbed "quit lit." These stories, told in blogs and columns of publications such as *The Chronicle of Higher Education*, "transform the act of quitting into a political process whereby the subject abdicates its competitive rationality to embrace a fundamental loyalty to different values and principles" (Coin, 2017, p. 707).[11] If it is true, as Fleming suggests, that "everything about us that isn't quantifiable is now desperately searching for a way out," then an exodus is perhaps to be expected (2021, p. 81). Ruth Barcan sees "a grave risk that rather than merely fighting for survival in the academy, more and more people will choose to thrive outside it" (2017, n.p.).

Quit lit thus raises issues of crucial relevance for the future of academia and—not least of all—the well-being of academics. As Barcan argues in *Academic Life and Labour in the New University: Hope and Other Choices* (2013):

> The serious questions raised by academics about how healthy, viable and prosperous a life a prospective academic might have within a university are […] grave interrogations of the intellectual and personal sustainability of a mass system organized around exploitative labour, whether that be the precarious labour of the ever-increasing casual staff or the overwork of the diminishing tenured staff. Such questions concern us doubly—as they bear on both the individual welfare of thousands of workers and the higher education system's capacity to systematically, impartially and carefully generate knowledge into the future. (p. 217)

By publicly voicing discontent with the status quo, the authors of quit lit lay down a "stepping stone in a collective discourse that ought to transform an inner conflict into a political alternative" (Coin, 2017, p. 708). *Collective* is the operative word here, because no matter what solutions we may find for ourselves at the individual level, lasting change at the institutional level requires collective action.

It is indicative of a culture of silence that the salutary effects of quit lit are achieved only after individual academics have made an exit. Thus far, there has been less discussion of work environment problems from within universities (a kind of 'stay lit,' if you will), but this, too, is a conversation that we as a profession need to have.

3   Solidarity as an Antidote

Academic workers are "remarkably lousy at translating their frustration into a sustained movement," as Fleming laments (2021, p. 9). Yet recent years have seen examples of successful collective action by academic workers in the United States and the United Kingdom. Some of these have taken a page from the playbooks of other professions. "The university's culture of individualism [...] mitigated against academics' collective action for a while," explains Jaffe, "but as the conditions of academic workers began more and more to resemble those of those other workers, academic workers began to reach for the tool of the working class: labor unions" (2021, p. 173).

A good example of the crucial role of collegial solidarity in the face of power abuse is found in a Swedish television documentary from 2021 about whistleblowers whose employers had retaliated against them. Train driver Ola Brunnström was threatened with termination after criticizing, in his role as union representative, the company for which he worked. We see him entering the meeting at which his future hangs in the balance, cheered on by co-workers protesting his firing by threatening to strike. Their message was heard by those in power, and Brunnström kept his job. "It's an emotional roller-coaster to be fired one day and have your job saved by your colleagues the next," he says in the documentary. "This show of solidarity also rescued me personally, my psyche and well-being. If you are alone and try to fight a battle without back-up, things can end badly. But sometimes you feel that you simply must fight" (Sveriges Television, 2021).[12]

Academic workers would do well to heed the wisdom of Ola Brunnström. Abuse of power in academia *can* be counteracted if we confront it collectively. "If we are even partly responsible for creating institutional dynamics," as Parker J. Palmer argues, "we possess some degree of power to alter them" (2017, p. 206). It does not always have to be the same old story. By working to overcome the divisive effects of the individualistic, ego-driven and hyper-competitive academic workplace, by forming coalitions and community, we can build a kinder and more sustainable work environment. For the creation of such a movement, giving voice to our experiences in stories like these is just the first step.

Notes

1   Damrosch (1995) also notes the normalization of deviant behavior within academia: "The sociologists who discuss behavioral patterns among academics speak quite directly about the unusual—or even deviant—nature of the contemporary academic personality. Thus, Michael Cohen and James March describe academic modes of decisionmaking as

'pathological'; but this is not a criticism, for they simply see such pathologies as the norms of an abnormal world [...] Seeking an analogy to campus patterns of interaction, another sociologist refers matter-of-factly to prisons" (p. 105). Damrosch concludes: "We should not remain content with a state of affairs that leads sociologists to compare universities as a matter of course to prisons and mental asylums" (p. 107).

2   The phenomenon of workplace bullying was first studied by the Swedish psychologist Heinz Leymann (1992). For recent research on workplace bullying, see Einarsen et al. (2020), which defines it in the following way:

> Bullying at work means harassing, offending, socially excluding someone or negatively affecting someone's work. In order for the label bullying (or mobbing) to be applied to a particular activity, interaction or process it has to occur repeatedly and regularly [...] and over a period of time [...]. Bullying is an escalating process in the course of which the person confronted may end up in an inferior position becoming the target of systematic negative social acts. A conflict cannot be called bullying if the incident is an isolated event or if two parties of approximately equal "strength" are in conflict. (p. 26)

3   For statistics on the prevalence of bullying in higher education, see Keashley and Neuman (2010); Zabrodska and Kveton (2013).

4   Translated into English as "Science as a Vocation." I cite here Gordon C. Wells' translation.

5   Einarsen et al. (2007) identify three categories of destructive leadership: tyrannical, derailed and supportive–disloyal. The first two are associated with abusive behavior toward subordinates, while the third shows concern about "the welfare of subordinates while violating the legitimate interest of the organization" (p. 213).

6   Davies (2005) summarizes the effects of neoliberalism in the following way: "a move from social conscience and responsibility towards an individualism in which the individual is cut loose from the social; from morality to moralistic audit-driven surveillance; from critique to mindless criticism in terms of rules and regulations combined with individual vulnerability to those new rules and regulations, which in turn press towards conformity to the group" (p. 12).

7   For a definition of the precariat, see Standing (2011). Jaffe writes:

> Increasing enrollment has not come along with increased full-time staffing, and salaries have stagnated as class sizes have increased. While European universities still offer more security than many US institutions, the situation of part-time faculty in the Americas [...] is a bellwether for the rest of the world. By 1999, an estimated one-fifth to one-half of European countries' academic staff were "nonpermanent." In the United States between 1975 and 2003, according to the AAUP, "full-time tenured and tenure-track faculty members fell from 57 percent of the nation's teaching staffs to 35 percent, with an actual loss of some two thousand tenured positions." (2021, p. 171)

8   Jonathan Malesic (2022) defines burnout as "the experience of being pulled between expectation and reality at work" (p. 12). His own experience as a tenured professor prompted him to write the book entitled *The End of Burnout: Why Work Drains Us and How to Build Better Lives*.

9   On the topic of academic imposter syndrome, see the chapter "Feeling Like a Fraud: Or, the Upside of Knowing You Can Never Be Good Enough" in Barcan (2013). Chapter 10 in the current book, by McGinnis, Núñez and Anonymous 4, touches on imposter syndrome and academia's "expectation of unfaltering passion."

10 On the role of shame in power abuse, see Lewis 2004. On the risks associated with a culture of silence in the workplace, see Edmondson (2019).

11 For a study of quitting as a response to workplace bullying, see Lutgen-Sandvik (2006).

12 My own translation of the Swedish transcript, which is available here: https://www.svt.se/ nyheter/granskning/ug/ug-referens-hall-kaften-och-lyd

References

Barcan, R. (2013). *Academic life and labour in the new university: Hope and other choices.* Ashgate.

Barcan. R. (2017, July 13). Universities need to plan for a dark future if academics prefer their own Plan B. *Times Higher Education.* https://www.timeshighereducation.com/ features/universities-need-to-plan-for-dark-future-if-academics-prefer-their-own-plan-b

Barcan, R. (2018). Paying dearly for privilege: Conceptions, experiences and temporalities of vocation in academic life. *Pedagogy, Culture & Society, 26*(1), 105–121.

Coin, F. (2017). On quitting. *Ephemera: Theory & Politics in Organization, 17*(3), 705–719.

Damrosch, D. (1995). *We scholars: Changing the culture of the university.* Harvard University Press.

Davies, B. (2005). The (im)possibility of intellectual work in neoliberal regimes. *Discourse: Studies in the Cultural Politics of Education, 26*(1), 1–14.

Edmondson, A. C. (2019). *The fearless organization: Creating psychological safety in the workplace for learning, innovation, and growth.* Wiley.

Einarsen, S., Aasland, M. S., & Skogstad, S. (2007). Destructive leadership behaviour: A definition and conceptual model. *Leadership Quarterly, 18,* 207–216.

Einarsen, S. V., Hoel, H., Zapf, D., & Cooper, C. L. (2020). *Bullying and harassment in the workplace: Theory, research and practice* (3rd ed.). CRC Press.

Fleming, P. (2021). *Dark academia: How universities die.* Pluto Press.

Jaffe, S. (2021). *Work won't love you back: How devotion to our jobs keeps us exploited, exhausted, and alone.* Bold Type Books.

Keashly, L., & Neuman, J. H. (2010). Faculty experiences with bullying in higher education: Causes, consequences, and management. *Administrative Theory & Praxis, 32*(1), 48–70.

Lewis, D. (2004). Bullying at work: The impact of shame among university and college lecturers. *British Journal of Guidance & Counseling, 32*(3), 281–299.

Leymann, H. (1992). *Från mobbning till utslagning i arbetslivet.* Publica.

Lutgen–Sandvik, P. (2006). Take this job and ...: Quitting and other forms of resistance to workplace bullying. *Communication Monographs, 73*(4), 406–433.

Malesic, J. (2022). *The end of burnout: Why work drains us and how to build better lives.* University of California Press.

Palmer, P. J. (2017). *The courage to teach: Exploring the inner landscape of a teacher's life* (20th anniversary ed.). Jossey–Bass.

Standing, G. (2011). *The precariat: The new dangerous class*. Bloomsbury Academic.

Sveriges Television. (2021). Håll käften och lyd. *Uppdrag granskning*. https://www.svt.se/nyheter/granskning/ug/ug-referens-hall-kaften-och-lyd

Thornton, M. (2004). Corrosive leadership (or bullying by another name): A corollary of the corporatized academy? *Australian Journal of Labour Law, 17*, 161–184.

Weber, M. (2008). Science as a vocation. In *Max Weber's complete writings on academic and political vocations* (J. Dreijamanis, Ed.; G. C. Wells, Trans.; pp. 25–52). Algora Publishing. (Original work published 1917)

Westhues, K. (2004). Editor's introduction. In K. Westhues (Ed.), *Workplace mobbing in academe: Reports from twenty universities* (pp. iii–vi). Edwin Mellen Press.

Zabrodska, K. (2013). Prevalence and forms of workplace bullying among university employees. *Employee Responsibilities and Rights Journal, 25*, 89–108.

Zabrodska, K., Linnell, S., Laws, C., & Davies, B. (2011). Bullying as intra-active process in neoliberal universities. *Qualitative Inquiry, 17*(8), 709–719.

www.ingramcontent.com/pod-product-compliance
Lightning Source LLC
Chambersburg PA
CBHW050530270326
41926CB00015B/3156